# UNFORGETTABLE

# UNFORGETTABLE

## New Rules for Business Storytelling

### ELAINE BRAMMER

GREAT STORIES®

Mill Creek, WA
Great Stories, Inc.

Unforgettable:
New Rules for Business Storytelling

Edited by Adam Finley
Illustrations by Sarah Xanthakis

Published by Great Stories
15710 24th Drive SE
Mill Creek, WA 98012
GreatStories.com

LCCN: 2023940819
ISBN: 9781662940422

Printed in the United States of America

*To Bill*

# CONTENTS

# INTRODUCTION

HOW DOES STORYTELLING differ from traditional content? Let me show you. Below is the exact same product presented in two different ways. Both are summary statements. Which one is the story?

> Option A: "Remote power management uses cloud-based analytics to schedule proactive maintenance and provide reliable power to clinics, keeping refrigerators running and protecting valuable vaccines."

> Option B: "Now, because of Product X, a grateful mother no longer worries whether her children will survive the next diphtheria epidemic."

Two types of content. Two wildly different levels of impact. Interestingly, it's not about length. Option A *feels* really long because it is neither cohesive nor compelling. Option B is a mere three words shorter, yet it is far more powerful. It has nothing to do with presentation—both options offer a single written sentence without the benefit of video, audio, or graphics. There is no difference in the efficacy or value of the product—it's the same product.

Every day, corporations choose what type of marketing content to create. They can build information-laden pieces packed with key messages, or they can create a human story. There is no middle ground that does both justice. Ideally, corporations create both kinds of content really, really well—but in order to do that, they have to know the difference.

It seems a simple question: What makes a story a story? Yet the business world has struggled to adopt a workable definition. And without a clear view of the target, it's impossible to hit the mark. How can you hope to craft compelling stories when the terminology is so fuzzy?

I'm going to clear that up for you. In the following pages, you will find a precise definition of business storytelling. You will also learn when to tell a story, when not to, and how to make storytelling work in a new context. Because context matters. A lot.

Storytelling in the business world does not equate to storytelling in the publishing world, yet we have failed to recognize the difference. Marketers have struggled long and hard to pluck the very best storytelling advice from the publishing arena and apply it to the corporate stage—and that creates a problem. The world of business is so dramatically different from the world of novels that we need to reshape the approach. To keep the parts that fit, trim the parts that don't, and uncover new knowledge to fill the gaps. Storytelling techniques must be customized to perform well on a new stage.

Novelists and how-to authors aren't immersed in a tug-of-war between case study production and authentic storytelling. They aren't juggling a 90-second time slot in an event agenda with the overarching goal of driving sales. They don't need to reach different audiences at various altitudes, and they don't battle against firmly entrenched yet classically dull marketing lingo. Perhaps most important, they don't face the same type of political battles.

Content is not created on an island. Marketing, sales, product, legal, and executive teams all vie for input based on their own priorities—and that's not even counting demands from the customer. Anyone who has worked in marketing knows that it takes years of experience to develop enough institutional knowledge to make headway. And that it's ridiculously difficult to align all of the competing forces in order to cross the finish line with an authentic human story.

The approach to business storytelling is out of kilter. Despite countless books, blogs, and presentations, proven advice that tackles the how-to side of business storytelling is in short supply. Unique business challenges haven't been addressed. Appropriate usage hasn't been defined. Storytelling has been presented as a universally applicable tool rather than one that requires selective, informed treatment. Despite a ton of chatter, there's not much clarity.

Storytellers need a new, customized set of rules that match the complexity of the corporate environment. They need guidance that goes beyond repurposed tips-and-tricks that tackle a tiny piece of the challenge, ignoring all of those vexing business hurdles along the way.

It's time to lay a new foundation. To design a unique approach that fills in the gaps and answers the tough business questions. When is a story the right approach, and when is traditional content better? Whose attention will you capture with a story, and who will be left in the dust? How do you knock down all of those frustrating hurdles between you and the finish line? What defines a story, anyway? And how do you create a captivating tale that is truly inspirational?

The purpose of this book is to move the needle. To make real, measurable progress by reducing the chatter and replacing it with *thorough*, *practical*, and *systematic* guidance that works in the business world.

- **Thorough** – This is more than a book about storytelling. It's a comprehensive look at how to successfully apply storytelling to the complex world of business. Sure, our conversation will include creative techniques. We will dig into plot lines, word choice, video skills, and how to hook your audience at the beginning and hold them all the way to the end.

  But that's not all. For example, you will learn how to predict when a storytelling approach will succeed and when it will backfire. You will unravel the mysteries of how a story will impact the audience, and determine how to objectively measure that impact.

- **Practical** – Here I will provide seasoned guidance on how to recognize and tackle all of those corporate-specific challenges. This is practical, on-the-ground, how-to advice. You will learn how to anticipate and finesse your way through review cycles, unclear expectations, hazy communications, customer complications, legal hassles, and frantic keynote requests. This is the information you need to help your story cross the finish line.

- **Systematic** – This book is broken down into logical areas of study. You can tackle all of it or part of it, depending on your role.

Part 1 lays the groundwork for a deeper understanding of corporate storytelling. Here you will find the foundational knowledge to inform both strategy and execution. Everyone from the C-Suite to marketing, public relations, and sales teams will find answers to their big questions. What *exactly* is storytelling? How does it impact the bottom line? Can someone finally clarify the difference between a case study and a story? Are stories always better than traditional content, or does it depend on the audience?

Part 1 will fill in knowledge gaps, bring your target into focus, and help you make informed decisions about how, where, and when storytelling fits into your content strategy.

Part 2 is nitty-gritty instruction for reviewers and storytelling practitioners—the folks who actually create the content. This is where you will find prescriptive guidance to improve your storytelling technique. Do you need practical instruction on how to formulate the best storyline? New skills to help you define your hero? Advice on holding audience attention? Here we will cover everything from improving your writing skills to upping your video expertise.

If you want to improve your hands-on storytelling skills—or your ability to offer helpful feedback—Part 2 is for you.

Part 3 will help marketing, public relations, and communication teams find answers to their tough questions. How do you get a key customer to sign a release form? Negotiate your way past features and benefits to a compelling storyline? Finesse your way to legal approval? How do you get all of the internal factions pulling in the same direction long enough to publish a compelling story?

If you count "story production" in your job description, Part 3 is for you. It will put the final touches on your storytelling skills and help you clinch your next project.

And finally, you will find a segment called "Fingertip reminders" after each major section. This is not meant to be a replacement for reading the section. As a matter of fact, it may not make sense without having first read the detail, but it will provide you with a readily-accessible reminder. And if you still have questions or find you need a deeper review, just flip back to the preceding section.

Now we're ready to get started. Through ten-plus years of navigating the murky waters of business storytelling, I have built and polished a new, end-to-end approach that has helped me create award-winning stories for Fortune 100 companies. Today, I'm excited to share it with you. In the following pages you will learn new methods and techniques to help you create inspirational brand stories that customers love, remember, and share.

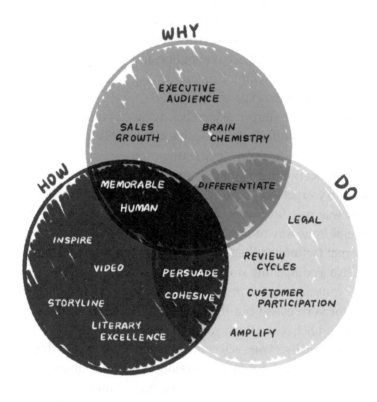

# PART 1
## ENVISION THE GOAL

HAVE YOU EVER wondered if storytelling is worth all the buzz? Why not just stick with traditional content? As with many business decisions, the answer lies in the bottom line—and a healthy bottom line relies on healthy sales. So how do you leverage your marketing expense to increase sales? Set the right goals.

Most high-level goals for content marketing sound something like this: Elevate brand awareness and perception in order to improve market position. Rephrased in street lingo it might sound like this: Inspire customers to think of our product first, recognize it as best, and choose to buy it more often. And what type of content does the best job of reaching the most people with the most positive impression? Storytelling.

Sounds simple, right? Not really. Business storytelling is a unique skill. It cannot be reduced to a broad-brush tool that you simply layer over traditional content. There is no magic storytelling applicator that suddenly turns everything into a story.

Storytelling requires more judicious treatment. A more selective and informed application. Switching to more conversational language won't get you there. Neither will simply creating a beginning, middle, and end to your content. The storyteller must understand exactly *what* storytelling is, *why* it can be a powerful tool, *who* will feel its pull, and *how* to execute it properly.

Our first job will be to deconstruct different types of content. We will start with the why, the who, and the what, and leave the how for later. *Why* are you creating a piece of content? *Who* is the target audience? And *what* is the defining structure? This will help you delineate between a story and any other asset. First up, let's take a closer look at a staple of the marketing world: the ever-popular case study.

# THE UBIQUITOUS
# CASE STUDY

*"If you only have a hammer, you tend to see every problem as a nail."*

—Abraham Maslow

YOU CAN LEARN a lot from nomenclature. If your purview is limited to marketing, you may think case studies are a marketing thing. Today, yes they are. But not exclusively. And historically, no. They were definitely not a marketing thing.

French scientist Frederic LePlay developed case studies in order to study finance in the 1800s. It was a new research tool, and it caught on. By the early 1900s, the case study had gained popularity at The University of Chicago,[1] where the Department of Sociology expanded its usage to the social sciences. A sociologist might, for example, use a case study to evaluate why a young adult male is unable to sleep in his new apartment. Or perhaps to determine the effect of mainstream education on an individual with learning disabilities.

Broadly speaking, case studies are an established research tool that is used in a variety of disciplines, particularly in the social sciences. Once the research is complete, the final step is to create a case study report. In simplified form, it looks like this:

- Background
- Problem Statement (Situation)
- Solution
- Results
- Conclusion

Look familiar? The sciences, of course, require a more expansive report than a marketing piece. The background includes more context. The problem statement calls out the questions that must be answered. The analytical tools are explained. There are more sections. More detail. But in essence, the format is the same. *The business world simply borrowed the research-based case study report and applied it to marketing.*

I don't know who first applied a case study methodology to marketing—I'm picturing a scientist in the midst of a radical career change—but it was genius. Case studies provide a reputable way to take a validated product experience with a positive outcome and communicate it to the world.

The approach has been largely successful, but also widely misunderstood. For many companies, case studies have become the default for customer content. Instead of adding a tool to the marketing arsenal, case studies have become *the* tool to share a customer experience. Sort of like a toolbelt with all hammers and no drill.

Sometimes a case study is the right answer, but choosing the very best type of content to resonate with a particular audience using a particular message for a particular reason is far more nuanced. There's a bit of faulty logic in the "all case studies all the time" approach. Case studies speak to some of the people some of the time, but they don't speak to all of the people all of the time. In fact, the audience for case studies is quite narrow.

So here we go—it's time to look at the why, the who, and the what of case studies. Then we will do the same for stories and compare the two, so you can more easily choose the right tool for the job.

## The right tool for the job

The first question you should ask yourself when creating a piece of content is why you are creating it. You won't be able to pick the right tool until you have a good handle on the job, so let's start by figuring out the purpose.

Broadly speaking, you have two choices. Marketing content typically fits into one of two buckets—it's either *informational* or *inspirational*. There's a bit of stylistic crossover, but only one primary purpose.

Toward the top of the sales funnel is where the inspirational content enters the picture. This is where you will find those compelling stories that grab your attention and hold it from beginning to end. The ones you become invested in. The ones you remember.

As you get closer to the bottom of the funnel, that's where you will find the informational assets. *Case studies fit into the informational bucket.* I know, I know—marketers have been working frantically for years to do the exact opposite. To somehow turn case studies into engaging, full-funnel stories complete with drama and victory. To meld the two separate types of content into a piece of Franken-content that serves both purposes.

I would advise against that approach. One-size-fits-all is not better than a targeted asset. Maintaining two different types of content—case study and story—is important for a couple of reasons:

1. Case studies may not make a big splash, but they serve a unique purpose. Salespeople rely on case studies to help close the deal, because they're packed with all the granular detail customers need to make a purchase decision. How easy was it to implement? What was the percent reduction in processing time? How much money was saved? When it's decision time, customers might shed a few tears over a great story, but they base their purchase decision on proven results.

2. Merging case studies and stories doesn't work. In fact, it's counterproductive. Not only will the attempt weaken the case, but it won't be a great story either. The elements that characterize a case study are destructive to a story. A rigid structure. Acronyms and industry terms. Facts and figures. Features and benefits.

Despite your best efforts, you can't remake a hammer into a drill. Rebranding the case study as a customer story won't make any difference. Adding an executive summary will not do the trick. A snazzy new template won't do it either. And if you do manage to throw equal parts inspiration and information into the same piece, you will find yourself the proud owner of an all-in-one hammerdrill that doesn't do either job well.

Now before you protest too loudly, there are a slew of look-and-feel tweaks that can be applied to a case study with great success. Add-ons and upgrades such as executive summaries, conversational language, pull quotes, photographs, and updated fonts can make a case study far more enjoyable to consume, so by all means use them! And if there's a compelling human element to a solution, it's a great aspect to call out in the case study. But as long as your primary focus is to document a customer's experience with a product and show their awesome results supported by a bunch of metrics and stats, it's not likely to turn into a tearjerker. Your audience will thank you for a smoother read if you use some of these techniques, but none of them have the power to be a shapeshifter.

In the end, a case study will remain a case study. That's okay. There's no need to make it into something it's not. The role of a case study is to educate and inform potential customers on the efficacy of your product. To analyze a business problem and the successful results (or the disastrous ones but nobody writes those) credited to a product or service. It's best told through the eyes of a customer and is designed to support decision-making. Done well, a case study provides the final evidence that compels your customer to sign on the dotted line.

That's the value of case studies. They provide business decision makers with a compelling use case that tips the purchase decision in your direction instead of your competitor's.

## Who cares?

Well it looks like I have let the cat out of the bag, but in my defense it was a little hard not to reveal the business decision maker (BDM) as the audience for a case study. BDMs are the folks tasked with choosing which product their company should buy. Chances are, no one else will care. That's the way it is with case studies—they have a narrow audience, often with a technical bent.

It makes sense. After all, the *only* reason to read a case study about telemetric blood pressure cuffs is if you are in the market for a telemetric blood pressure cuff. The same is true for pneumatic temperature controllers, automated camera dollies, and cloud-based machine learning tools. I could probably understand a case study on any of those topics, but I won't be curling up with any of them on a Sunday afternoon.

Although not everyone will care to read a case study, those in the market for your product may care a lot. They *need* the information to help them make a decision. Who has used the product before? Did they use it in a scenario similar to mine? What were the results? Can you give that to me in hard numbers? In the end, were they satisfied? And would they recommend the product?

If you are hoping to use a customer experience to influence BDMs to choose your product, then by all means create a case study. Call out a business problem and how your company was able to solve it, then be sure to wow them with a lot of metrics.

On the other hand, if you want to have the broadest possible reach and create a seismic shift in brand perception, a case study won't do the trick. So before you put your fingers to the keyboard, be sure to ask yourself why you are creating the content and who will care to read it.

## What makes a case study a case study?

So what does a case study look like and how do you build one? Is there a defining structure common to case studies? It turns out there is—and it's quite rigid, which is not a surprise given its roots in research methodology.

A case study narrative is linear. Flat. Similar to a documentary. Case studies relay events in a formulaic, sequential fashion.

Check out this fictional case study from ScreaminFastData™:

- Background:
  - ➤ Consumers are increasingly shopping online and making mobile payments.
  - ➤ The mobile payment market is approaching $2.1 trillion globally.
  - ➤ Credit card fraud exceeds $30 billion globally and is expected to double in 10 years.
  - ➤ SmokinFastPay™ (customer) is the largest payment processing provider in the world.
- Problem:
  - ➤ Consumers demand speed and security for their payments, whether in person, online, or using a smartphone.
- Solution:
  - ➤ SmokinFastPay deployed a revolutionary new cloud-based data platform by ScreaminFastData.
- Results:
  - ➤ Transaction speeds improved by 23%.
  - ➤ Security breaches decreased by 69%.
- Conclusion:
  - ➤ ScreaminFastData solved SmokinFastPay's business problem (and it can solve yours too).

Visually, the narrative flow looks like the diagram below. You can see the flat, linear, sequential progression. There's no universal, life-changing, anxiety-producing conflict to bend the curve. Nothing to raise your blood pressure. And no, things like processing speed or improved efficiency don't qualify as a human conflict. Those are metrics and stats.

## CASE STUDY NARRATIVE

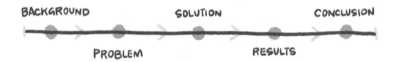

A flat narrative structure isn't necessarily a bad thing. In this case, it's the right tool for the job. Case studies are your opportunity to add absolute, unequivocal science to the purchase decision. You simply lead the customer from Point A to Point B across flat ground and ring up the sales at the end.

## All about the numbers

Case studies hinge on numbers. A *lot* of numbers. Impressive numbers. The more substantial the numbers, the better the case study.

Numbers make or break the case. This is where you unequivocally *prove* the efficacy of your product or service. Numbers to show the imposing size of your customer. Numbers to validate increased efficiencies and reduced costs. Ultimately, numbers that will lock up the decision to buy. With numbers like these, how can they refuse?

- 3 billion transactions annually
- $37.2 billion in global sales
- 24% improvement in processing time

- $22.8 million dollars saved annually
- 18% faster to market

Often customers will readily share their own "About" numbers such as annual revenue or global footprint, but are more timid about numbers tied to the success of your product. Your customer might insist on vague comments like these:

- Improved safety and reliability
- New data insights
- Reduced downtime
- Dynamic updates
- Scalable solutions

Generalities are far from ideal, so good marketers push for numbers. If the customer isn't comfortable with citing a dollar amount, they may be okay with a percentage, or with the inclusion of "as much as" before the statistic. Hefty, finite numbers are the mark of a good case study. This is the proof that your company's product or service can do the job and do it well.

## This year's style

Case studies are sort of like the news—old-fashioned Walter Cronkite style. Information, information, information. Stories are more like a *Grey's Anatomy* rerun. Laughter, tears, more laughter. Cronkite would have been *really* awkward in Grey's Anatomy, and Meredith Grey would have been equally out-of-place in a Cronkite-style news program. Today the line between news and sitcom is considerably murkier, but that's another story. (It does, however, explain why I had to rely on an antiquated news example.) Still, case studies are built to convey information while stories speak to the heart.

Despite the wide difference in form and function, there's often an overlap in look-and-feel. There's no need to deploy overly stiff language in a case study. You won't seem more credible, and the numbers won't be more reliable. It's not like you can trick them into thinking you're revealing secrets from behind locked doors. We all understand that a case study conveys validated information regarding the efficacy of a product.

Still, a BDM will appreciate a more fluid writing style as long as you keep a professional tone. An executive summary is polite and much-appreciated. Images can make the whole experience more pleasant. Pull quotes bring the most relevant quotes to the forefront and break up the monotony of the page. All of these tweaks will make a written case study more consumable, as long as they support the purpose of the case study: to educate and inform.

## Ooh . . . how about a video?

So far we've talked about written case studies. But what about video? Videos are popular, but they're also expensive. You can only fit so many topnotch videos into a budget, and there's not much point in making a lousy one. It might even set you back. *The quality of a marketing asset can reflect as heavily on the product as the messaging.* Why would I believe in the excellence of your product if your video is far from excellent? A second-rate video (or case study or presentation) won't leave a positive impression regardless of how well the product performed.

Videos also take a ton of time. There's typically an agency involved. More release forms. Travel. Editing. And in the end, a case study video is not necessarily more compelling than a well-written piece. After all, you're constrained by the very nature of the content—content that is so rigid that it might not justify the cost.

This is how a case study video usually goes:

1. **Introduce the customer**—queue the ever-popular "establishing shot" of a branded sign.

2. **Show some context**—maybe hallway or conference room shots with people engaged in business conversation. Some stuff on a whiteboard. And here's where the talking heads come in to talk about their challenge.

3. **Explain the solution**—probably a good time for over-the-shoulder screenshots. Ideally a mobile device or two. Lab or manufacturing floor shots are nice. More talking heads.

4. **List the results**—it's time for the execs to talk about the great results they attained. Maybe some kinetic text to hammer home the point.

5. **Hit the big close**—pile together all of your best summary quotes from the folks with the most impressive titles. Done.

We have all suffered through a million case study videos that look exactly alike. Why are they so darn cookie-cutter? Because case studies are hardwired that way. It's easy to understand once you have seen the rigid, pre-set structure. *How on earth could you break the mold when it's the mold that defines the content?* It's even more obvious once you realize that the best case studies are overburdened with metrics and numbers that would exhaust all but the most dedicated decision-makers.

## About that video budget

There is no need to duplicate the written case study in video form. In my opinion, you're better off to save your dollars for a handful of knock-out storytelling videos—those deeply human stories that are captivating, inspirational, and memorable. You can spend four times as much per video, create one-fourth as many videos, and make a bigger splash if you use your video budget to produce great stories.

My experience is that high-impact storytelling videos will be used over...and over...and over again. You can use them everywhere—events, customer meetings, conferences, web pages, social media—because they're broad-audience assets that appeal to everyone. You can even show them to decision-makers to grab their attention right before you slide the written case study across the table. Videos that tell human stories are a dynamite resource and well worth the investment.

 **Fingertip reminders**

In summary, when it's time for decision-making, case studies are the tool for the job. They may not be tear-jerkers, but they sell. I would rather buy a product that's 73% effective than one that's 52% effective, and so would your customer. And it's a pretty good bet they would rather hear it from the mouth of a happy customer than from you. Over two-thirds of B2B marketers create case studies and use them to nurture leads and convert them to sales.[2] That's a mighty important reason to create a piece of content.

Here's what we have learned so far:

- Case studies are informational. They provide the granular detail customers need to make a purchase decision.

- Trying to turn a case study into a story doesn't work. The elements that characterize a case study (rigid structure, facts and figures, features and benefits) are destructive to a story.

- Case studies rely on hard numbers (40% lower cost, 1.7x more productive).

- Why – The purpose of a case study is to tip the purchase decision in your direction instead of your competitor's.

- Who – Case studies provide valuable information to business decision makers (BDMs).

- What – The narrative flow is flat, linear, and sequential.

## CASE STUDY NARRATIVE

BACKGROUND          SOLUTION              CONCLUSION

PROBLEM                    RESULTS

- Case study videos tend to be formulaic and may not provide the greatest return on your investment. Instead, save the majority of your video budget for storytelling.

# THE REAL STORY

*"A great lasting story is about everyone or it will not last. The strange and foreign is not interesting—only the deeply personal and familiar."*

—John Steinbeck

WITH CASE STUDIES, it's all about the numbers. With stories, it's all about a changed life. Let's start with an everyday comparison. Anyone who has ever received a new baby phone call knows the drill:

Lucy went into labor last night. We headed to the hospital when her contractions were five minutes apart. The hospital staff was great. It was pretty crazy for a while, but once the epidural kicked in things were a lot better. Zoe was born at 6:12 this morning: 7 pounds 3 ounces, 19 inches long, and beautiful. Mom and baby are doing great.

There it is: Situation – Solution – Results. The telltale signs of a case study. The flat, documentary-style narrative used to relay information. I could have made it longer, but unless you're a hospital administrator you probably don't care what year the maternity suite was built. Or statistics on the percentage of male babies versus female. Or a brief bio on the attending physician.

Now back to baby Zoe. The information is nice to have, but those in the inner circle want to hear the "real" story. Something like this:

> We've been trying for so long to have a baby. Lucy's really excited, but she's terrified of labor and delivery. Her friends keep telling her horror stories about the pain and trauma. I wish they'd just shut up. When her best friend unexpectedly lost her baby last month, Lucy's fear and anxiety really amped up. Her doctor put her on meds, but I still wasn't sure how she'd handle it when we got to the real deal.
>
> Once Lucy's contractions were five minutes apart, we headed to the hospital. I could tell she was getting anxious, but the staff was amazing. When we checked in, right away they reassured her. Told her she was doing great. There was always someone there, coaching her and telling her everything would be fine.
>
> When the epidural kicked in, she really relaxed. And when they put the baby on her chest, oh man—I've never seen her so happy. Me too. Zoe was born at 6:12 this morning. She's 7 pounds 3 ounces, 19 inches long, and perfect.

Notice the difference? The story uses a human conflict to engage the audience and bring them along on the journey until it reaches a final resolution. Even though all the same information is included, the impact is completely different. Stories drive connection through the use of universal human emotions and experiences: fear, pain, excitement, love, joy.

Now we will dig into stories. First up is the why, the who, and the what.

## Why do stories matter anyway?

We create stories because they connect us at a human level. They're emotive. Memorable. They leverage shared emotions and experiences to place the speaker and audience on the same journey. We unite to cheer on the hero and rage at the villain, and we've been doing it for millennia.

From cave drawings to oral traditions to the printing press, humans have always been storytellers. We share our experiences, our culture, and our lives through story. We teach ethics and cultural norms. We use stories to overcome our fears and celebrate our victories—and we don't keep it to ourselves. Humans share stories in order to connect with other humans.

A business story is no different. Business stories provide a vehicle for human connection. They're inspirational, and as a consequence they have impact. A great story hits the audience in their gut. They think about it. Talk about it. Show it to others.

When that happens, your brand image clicks up a notch. Ideally, customers show their corporate teams and they ask: "What can we do to be part of this story?" That's the goal—to tell a story that is so universal, so human, and so compelling that your customer wants to be part of it.

If you tell great stories, everyone from the C-suite to the sales team will love you for it. Not because case studies stink and stories rock, but because *stories reach a broad audience at a deep level.* They engross people in your story, elevate brand image, fill the top of the unquenchable sales funnel, trickle all the way down to the bottom, and turn your solution into the one everyone is talking about.

That's the thing with good stories—they're magnetic. They attract an audience. The more universal the topic, the larger the audience. Once the audience is hooked, you have the power to pull them along until everyone is on the same page—which just so happens to be your page. A story gives you the opportunity to turn a compelling cause into your cause. One that you have the power to solve.

Stories are built on something everyone cares about. Hunger. Poverty. Education. Health. These are the universal topics that are easy to relate to. Everyone has felt hunger, although for the more fortunate it's a temporary annoyance. Yet we ache for those whose hunger and poverty have become a daily struggle. We wish everyone had the opportunity for a good education. And we understand the life-changing wallop of disease. These are the kinds of problems that everyone cares about, and they care a lot.

You may be thinking this all sounds grand, but it's a pipe dream for your industry. It's easy to tell a universal story if your product happens to solve poverty—not so much if you sell socket wrenches or shoelaces or forklifts.

Granted, not every piece will have touch points as broad and strong as world hunger, but you can usually find a way to make a product story more engaging. With a little digging you might be able to elevate a relatable issue such as urbanization, energy, or transportation above the facts and figures, then enfold the solution into the narrative.

## Everybody has a story

Several years ago I received a Microsoft case study nomination touting the benefits of cloud-based predictive models to reduce elevator downtime. The solution was pretty cool and I felt like the piece might have broad appeal, but not if we created a traditional case study. Elevators have widespread familiarity, but cloud-based remote management does not. I consulted with the CMO at the elevator company to see if there was another angle. He recommended we bump "urbanization" to the lede.

It was a great idea. Urbanization gave us the opportunity to craft a great opening line that established the migration from country to city as a challenge—and elevators to serve tall buildings as the solution. We set the opening against a backdrop of bustling sidewalks and crowded streets. It worked. The migration from farm to city had been going on for centuries. Everybody knew it, it was affecting daily lives, and it had changed the skyline—making buildings taller and elevator reliability more critical.

Granted, it wasn't exactly a cliffhanger, but it was way more interesting than a traditional case study with a Situation—Solution—Results format. In fact, it was interesting enough to land in multiple Microsoft keynote addresses.

When you are staring at information, remember to back up a bit and see if you can find a topic that a lot of people care about. If so, you can shift from a linear, informative piece to an inspirational piece. It's a winning strategy, because when you become the problem-solver, you also become the hero. Your company is now the one to turn to in order to solve the hard problems. The ones everyone cares about.

The approach may sound contrived, but it's not. Not for the solutions I care about and probably not the ones you care about either. As marketers we tend to have a narrow, product-focused lens. Features and benefits. Problems and personas. E-books and social snippets. Blogs for the media savvy, case studies for the business decision makers, white papers for the most technical audience. And all along the way we are promoting narrow-focused reasons to use our product.

Stories allow us to expand our audience and deepen the connections. They join our story with their story and let us share in the triumph together. It's the difference between sitting quietly at a hard desk alone in a cold room (case study), and chatting with close friends beside a cozy fire (story). The difference between absorbing information and forming a connection.

## Who cares?

The key to finding the *who* is to look back at the *why*, because the two attributes are inextricably linked. Once you determine *why* you are creating a piece of content, you will find the *who* practically answers itself. Still, it's important to call it out and to keep the audience in the forefront of your mind during the creative process. *Knowing your audience is key to creating great content.* It will affect your choice of storyline, language, and tone.

When we examined case studies, it became obvious that they provide the information needed to support decision making. Bam. The audience is a business decision maker. With stories, we have moved from informational content to inspirational content. Stories reach a much broader audience because they explore universal themes at a human level. Remember this line? — "Stories drive connection through the use of *universal human* emotions and experiences: fear, pain, excitement, love, joy." There's your answer. Everyone relates to a good story.

The best stories are relatable to every human walking the earth. They're captivating, emotive, inspiring, and memorable. A case study audience is determined by business role, but a story audience has no such boundary. *Stories are for everyone.*

Stories give you the opportunity to position your product as the solution that solves the biggest problems for the most people. They take your brand voice and crank up both the bandwidth and the volume. Suddenly your narrow-audience solution is relevant.

Next up, we will talk structure. This will help you to recognize a story and distinguish it from any other type of content. It will also set you on a path to be able to create your own.

## What makes a story a story?

We know that stories are inspirational and relatable to a broad audience. But *what* distinctly defines a story? What is its DNA?

First, we will clear up a bit of confusion between attributes— those qualities that might be shared among multiple types of content—and the structural DNA that sets a story apart from everything else. Descriptors can be helpful, but they aren't definitive.

For example, check out these attributes shared by the vast majority of cats—the ones that fit in the middle of the bell curve. We will leave those fringe breeds such as the furless Sphynx and the tailless Manx out of the picture for now.

- Furry
- Pointy ears
- Long tail
- Whiskers

And here are some descriptors for a dog. Again, we will ignore the furless and tailless varieties.

- Furry
- Floppy or pointy ears
- Long or short tail
- Whiskers

The overlap is confusing. The two lists make sense if I already know what a cat or a dog looks like, but are severely lacking if I have somehow managed to reach adulthood without seeing either species. If I were faced with seeing a dog and a cat for the first time, I would not be able to distinguish between the two.

We could add more detail such as longhair or shorthair, but that wouldn't help. Both dogs and cats have longhair and shorthair varieties. We could add size, but that gets confusing. If my comparative study entails putting a cougar and a Toy Poodle in the same room, I'm instantly confused. The poodle may have bigger problems.

In the end, *two completely different species might share the same attributes, but they're not the same animal.* However, it does explain why people get confused. It's not surprising. For example, the push for storytelling has been tumbling around marketing organizations for some time now. Stories routinely use conversational language and imagery. They have a more modern look-and-feel than a traditional case study. They're also more relatable. Without understanding the foundational differences, it might lead one to believe that applying these types of attributes—conversational language, imagery, modern look-and-feel—will transform a case study into a story.

Alas, no. While these qualities certainly make the content easier to digest, none of them uniquely define a particular type of content. Case studies have in recent years adopted a look-and-feel similar to stories, yet the DNA of a case study has not changed. It is still built on a flat, linear narrative.

Stories are different. Their DNA structure doesn't look the same at all. The foundation of a story follows the unique, telltale pattern of a story arc.

You can see what a story arc looks like in the diagram below. It starts off flat for just long enough to set up the story.

Once the audience has engaged and there's enough context for them to follow along, a conflict bends the curve upward. The more anxiety-producing the conflict, the steeper and higher the rise.

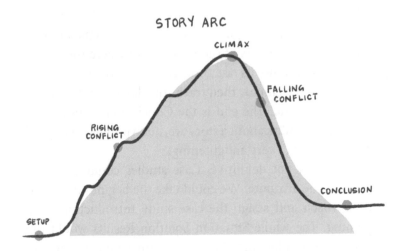

Good stories will often provide relief points on the ascent—a chance for the audience to catch their breath. Once you reach the climax, the arc turns dramatically downward. The peak typically occurs most of the way through the story, and the descent can be rapid. After all, once the hero fells the villain, the story is about over. Nobody wants to watch 45 minutes of happily ever after.

The relief points that interrupt the steep ascent aren't needed on the descent. Once the conflict is resolved, all we need to do is give the audience a bit of time to recover as we tie up loose ends and leave things nice and tidy.

You will notice the Conclusion ends at a different height than the Setup. That's not due to my lousy drawing skills, although it could be. The point of telling a great story is that you leave the audience at a different point than they began. Otherwise, why did you tell it?

Another description you might hear is that a story has a beginning, a middle, and an end. Although that is certainly true, I don't find the description particularly useful.

First, it's too vague. You have to dig quite a bit deeper to understand that the Beginning is typically thought of as the Setup. The middle starts at the initial bend where the conflict is introduced, follows its rise through various relief points and all the way to the climax, then tracks the descent until the final bend to horizontal. The end is the Conclusion. I suppose it's another way to think about a story arc, but without considerable elaboration it isn't very enlightening.

Second, it's not definitive. Case studies could be said to have the same attribute. We could take the beginning-middle-end approach and assign the case study Introduction as the beginning. The whole Situation-Solution-Results would then become the middle, and the Conclusion would be the end. Nothing about the beginning-middle-end description would clarify whether the structure is flat or curved.

Third, it infers a sequential progression through time. Stories aren't always built that way. Flashbacks and even flashforwards can be a powerful tool in the hands of a good storyteller.

In summary, case studies and stories are two different animals. They might have common attributes, but they vary widely in purpose, audience, and structure.

We create case studies to give BDMs the information that will tip the purchase decision in our direction. We lay it all out in an $A + B = C$ fashion. Nice, clean, and by the numbers.

We create stories because they're inspirational. They have the power to captivate a broad audience and bring them along on a journey through conflict and resolution. Ultimately, stories allow us to tie our brand to solutions that change the world.

Inspiration is a mighty lofty goal, but it's hard to measure. It's also hard to see how a story can possibly have that much impact on the audience. In the next chapter, we will explore the science behind storytelling and share an objective tool that makes it all a little less fuzzy. But before we go on, here are a few reminders.

 **Fingertip reminders**

Stories allow us to connect with a broad audience at a human level. They engross the audience, elevate brand image, fill the top of the unquenchable sales funnel, trickle all the way down to the bottom, and turn your solution into the one everyone is talking about. Good stories are compelling, emotive, and memorable.

Here's a list that will help define stories:

- Stories are inspirational.
- Case studies and stories may have common attributes such as conversational language and imagery, but they're distinctly different assets.
- Why – The purpose of a story is to expand the audience, create a human connection, and elevate brand image.
- Who – Stories are for everyone.
- What – The narrative flow of a story follows the telltale pattern of a story arc.

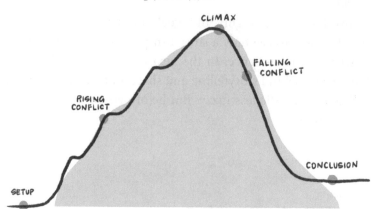

# THE STUDIOUS STORYTELLER

MARKETING IS ABOUT influence. Sure, we can put fancier words around it such as "build brand awareness," "improve conversion rates," or "establish thought leadership." We can set quarterly benchmarks for website traffic and contact sharing. We can even gin up a formula to estimate how many leads we need in order to achieve revenue goals. But in the end, marketing is an affective sport—if we don't sway impressions, we don't move the ball closer to the goal.

Our role as marketers is to figure out what type of content will have the most clout. We want to affect the most people in the strongest way possible. In order to reach that goal, we need to understand how our brain processes different types of content.

Science can help. In recent years researchers have begun to unravel the mystery around how our brains perceive and respond to stories. A number of fascinating discoveries have provided new clues about how our minds interpret stories. They also help to explain why stories capture us in a way that informational content cannot.

## The information limitation

As marketers, we are specialists in assembling, curating, and polishing information into carefully constructed messages. Then we weave those key messages into our content and pass the word: "Stay on message!" We don't want to confuse the customer, and repetition is our friend. It increases our chance that the audience will hear our message. But how well does the audience actually hear and remember the information we feed them? Once we throw it out there, how well does our messaging sink in?

The brain processes messaging as it would any other kind of information—by activating the posterior temporal lobe, specifically a spot known as Wernicke's area. Although somewhat more complicated, Wernicke's is the primary area responsible for language comprehension.[3] This is the same area that would assign meaning to any incoming information, such as a lecture on Napoleon Bonaparte or a YouTube video on how to get your cat to swallow medication.

## From candlelight to floodlight

Stories, on the other hand, have a much larger effect on the brain. With stories, familiar objects and experiences produce the same neural response as they would in real life. It's not just the language processing zone that gets activated by a story—huge portions of the brain light up.

Imagine you are reading about apples sprinkled with cinnamon and bubbling in the oven. If you have ever smelled cinnamon on a baked apple, the olfactory region in your brain will light up. Watch someone eat a banana onscreen? Now your visual system conjures up a banana, your motor system goes through the motions of grasping, peeling, and eating the banana, your olfactory system recalls the smell, and your gustatory system recreates the taste. Basically, when you think about a banana, your brain reenacts the scene real time.[4] If you haven't yet encountered the exact same scenario, your brain will extrapolate based on a similar experience. Replace the banana with an exotic fruit you've never tried, and your brain will still light up as though you're experiencing it.

Stories take advantage of these mental connections. Similes and metaphors may be figures of speech, but they illicit literal reactions in the brain. If you hear "his skin was as rough as sandpaper," your brain will reenact what it knows about sandpaper by activating the region of the brain that senses texture through touch.[5] The audience member responds by constructing the sights, sounds, smells, tastes, and touches of the narrative in their brain. In the end, the person who reads or listens to a story plays an active part in the tale.

But that's not all. If the serial killer follows the heroine as she walks home through a dark alley, the person watching the scene unfold will feel genuine fear.[6] Even though we *know* it isn't real, our minds will reenact the emotional response appropriate for the situation. So now the insular cortex has joined the game by throwing emotion into the mix. The insular cortex acts as an integration hub, receiving the sensory and cognitive signals, mixing in emotional processing, and spitting out full-fledged experiential responses to stories.[7] Have you ever jumped on cue in a movie? Tightened your muscles when the actor is in a precarious position? That's your insular cortex doing its job.

In terms of brain activity, there's little difference between reading a story and experiencing the actual event.[8] It's why we root for the hero and sob at the happy ending. *Their* story has become *our* story. It's also why watching a movie inspired by a favorite book can be so disappointing—you walk into the theater having already seen the movie in your mind. If the director's cut is significantly different, in your mind's eye it's "wrong." The movie industry took a perfectly good book and destroyed it. Again.

Now the science gets even weirder. When a speaker tells a story to a listener, the listener exhibits the same brain activity as the speaker—after a delay to allow for processing time, of course.[9] It's called neural coupling. When the speaker tells the story, the associated parts of his or her brain light up in response to whatever is going on in the story. One to three seconds later, the same areas light up in the listener's brain. As storytellers, we literally take the listener along for the ride. Talk about influence! Stories are the closest (legal) thing we have to mind control.

For millennia, humans have leveraged the deep mental connection of stories to draw others along on a journey. Storytelling allows us to form connections, share experiences, and generally make sense of the world.

Business stories have the same superpower—a quality that informational assets do not share. Stories are more captivating and resonate more deeply. They're more memorable than facts, figures, and ideas alone, and they're more likely to be shared and discussed. A good story will have impact long after the last scene fades.

## Predicting impact

Case studies are objective by nature, so predicting their impact is pretty easy. Typically the most impressive, quantifiable results from the biggest brands are reliably the strongest case studies. But what about a story? How can we objectively measure which stories might have the greatest impact?

It's pretty easy, really. I use a simple two-dimensional graphic that I call the "Impact Quadrant." The quadrant allows us to plot two parameters—Interest and Intensity—in order to quantify impact. Interest and Intensity are simply numbers assigned based on how *many* people are interested in a topic and how *much* they're interested.

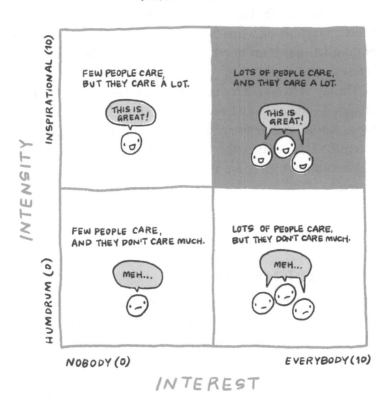

First, estimate how many people would reasonably be interested in a topic. Rank it from zero (nobody) to ten (everybody). Remember, the ideal is everyone. A topic like urbanization might rank a five or six, whereas health will land up in the nine-to-ten range.

Second, do the same for how much the audience will care—rank it from zero to ten. In general, people might care a bit about transportation, but they're likely to care a lot more about poverty.

You can see where this is going. The top-left quadrant will house the very few people who care intensely about Hungarian folk music of the 18th century, and the bottom-right quadrant will represent all the folks who care a tiny bit about people who insist on jaywalking when there's a crosswalk 50 feet away. The bottom-left quadrant doesn't rack up big numbers for either Interest or Intensity.

The key is to search for the stories that land in the top-right quadrant—the ones that everyone cares a lot about. Look for those stories that register six or above in *both* Interest and Intensity. This is where the great stories live. The ones that will make an impact. Here are a few reminders to help you in your search.

 **Fingertip reminders**

In recent years, a number of fascinating discoveries have provided new clues about how our minds interpret stories. They also help to explain why stories capture us in a way that informational content cannot.

- Informational content activates the brain's language processing zones.

- Stories activate any area of the brain that we would use if we were to actually experience the events of the story, including the areas that manage vision, smell, taste, touch, hearing, emotions, motor skills, *and* language processing.

- When the speaker tells a story, his or her brain lights up in response to whatever is going on in the story. One to three seconds later, the same areas light up in the listener's brain in a phenomenon known as neural coupling.

- The Impact Quadrant helps us quantify story impact by assigning numbers (0-10) to Interest and Intensity based on how *many* people care about a topic and how *much* they care. Really great stories will land in the top-right quadrant.

## IMPACT QUADRANT

# ODDS AND ENDS

N OW WE'RE GOING to hit a couple of final topics before we wind up the foundational elements of storytelling and move on to some practical advice.

## The nomenclature trap

Everyone has experienced conversations that go nowhere because the folks who are talking can't seem to get on the same wavelength. Each side keeps repeating themselves, often at a higher volume. Sometimes it's due to a genuine disagreement, but too often they're simply not speaking the same language. Words can mean different things to different people, or the same words might have different meanings in different situations. So how do we agree on content labels in order to have a lucid conversation about content?

The challenge is not an easy one. The industry has mired itself in a nomenclature trap so confusing it can make your head spin. A task as rudimentary as delineating between the *type* of content and the *form* of content is baffling.

Check out this typical list of (supposed) content types:

- Blog
- Video
- Case study

- Long-form content
- Podcast
- Infographic
- Whitepaper
- eBook
- Social media
- Webinar

Right off the bat I see *case study* and *video* listed separately. But case studies can be either written or video, so that's pretty confusing. As a matter of fact, listing video as a standalone asset makes no sense at all. Not only are case studies sometimes in video format, but so are webinars, social media posts, and stories.

Wait a minute—stories don't appear *anywhere* on the list even though they're distinctly different from every other entry. Perhaps it's because storytelling is treated as a stylistic technique, but we know that techniques such as conversational language and visuals don't change a case study into a story. So why is story not on the list?

And why is long-form on the list? Long-form is literally a descriptor for the length of content. Depending on who you ask, the crossover might be 1,200 words, or 4,000 words, or pretty much any other number between 1,000 and 10,000 words depending on the author and time of day.

We need a different way to classify and label content that defines both the type and the form. Some pieces are fairly easy, such as an infographic. As a matter of fact, that's the best handle I have ever seen on a piece of content. It's a dead giveaway! Infographics are *info*rmational assets in *graph*ic form. The name is a literal see-and-say.

A webinar is sort of like an online classroom for the business world. It's informational content in video form. But what about social media? Social media is literally just a platform to publish content—which could be informational or inspirational, and could be in the form of a video, or text, or graphic. It's so flexible that it's all over the map.

In any case, we need more than one organizational tier to adequately describe a piece of content. In my dictionary there are two parameters: type and form. The *type* of content comes in two flavors—informational or inspirational—and the *form* includes at least three options—written, video, and graphic. Like this:

| | Content Type | | Content Form | | |
|---|---|---|---|---|---|
| | *Informational* | *Inspirational* | *Written* | *Video* | *Graphic* |
| **Story** | | X | X | X | |
| **Case Study** | X | | X | X | |
| **Whitepaper** | X | | X | | |
| **eBook** | X | | X | | |
| **Infographic** | X | | | | X |
| **Social media** | X | X | X | X | X |
| **Webinar** | X | | | X | |
| **Blog** | X | (X) | X | | |

As you can see, we have a ton of informational options at our disposal, but far fewer inspirational pieces. A story is the one and only type of content that is forever and always inspirational.

A social media post might be inspirational depending on what it's promoting, but it will be too short to register very high on the Inspirometer™. And a blog could feasibly contain inspirational content, but that's not how they typically roll.

One of the keys to adopting a common language is the ability to recognize whether a piece of content is mainly inspirational or informational. Here is a quick checklist to help you figure out the correct bucket.

## Key Indicators for Informational Content

- Does it answer the questions a potential buyer might ask?
- Is it number-centric?
- Would it be easy to create a Key Learnings list from this content?
- Would it lend itself to an infographic?

## Key Indicators for Inspirational Content

- Would most people care about the topic?
- Would it stir an emotional response?
- Would they be likely to remember it?

Once we clear up the content type—informational or inspirational—the form will fall naturally into place. Now we have a common language we can use to talk about content strategy, including what type of assets we need and where they will live. We will be able to identify the holes more easily and pinpoint exactly where we should concentrate our efforts.

Some of those content holes may involve storytelling, and learning to create great stories will require exercising some muscles that may have been dormant for a while. After all, creating traditional content is a repetitive use activity. There's a bit of rinse-and-repeat applied to the method.

On the other hand, creating stories is definitely not rinse-and-repeat. It won't fit in a cookie-cutter mold. If you have lived in the marketing world for a while, you may need to rebuild your creative muscles to make any headway in storytelling. The next section will help you exercise those muscles.

## Creativity unleashed

Stories provide an opportunity for creativity that simply can't be matched by its informational cousins. Whitepapers are technical, formal, and detailed. Case studies are confined by a Situation – Solution – Results narrative. eBooks have platform limitations. Infographics are limited to a visual presentation. Social media is necessarily brief. Webinars are framed around an educational format. Podcasts are aural.

So many boundaries and so little wiggle room. With all the constraints, marketing content can become blasé—the same vocabulary used in the same formats to relay the same information. Without a fresh mindset, a new ask can quickly devolve into a robotic response.

Event, you say? Who's the keynote speaker? Easy. I'll refashion the latest messaging in the voice of the speaker, throw in a few personas specific to the audience, flesh it out with a customer example, and . . . done.

Webinar? Who's the speaker? Let me grab the latest messaging, turn it into a deep dive with the help of the product manager, overlay the speaker's voice, and . . . done.

Stories offer a fresh approach. As long as they introduce a human conflict and seek to resolve it, the rest is wide open. They can be written or video. Recorded or live. Short or long. One character or multiple characters. They can have a strict chronological timeline or use foreshadowing and echoes to heighten the suspense. The point of view can vary. So can the author's voice. The ending might employ a bookend or an open-end.

Stories open a whole world of creative options—maybe even a few things you haven't thought of trying in a business context. Granted, if you get too far off the beaten path you risk losing the audience. *Way* too far off and it might be a topic in your next review.

The trick is to shake the bars just hard enough to grab the audience's attention and land your point in a memorable fashion. You want to make it stick just a little bit stronger.

It can be easier said than done. A creative rut that has been worn deep can be tough to climb out of. Habits are that way— they gradually become such a strong go-to nudge that it's hard to think of any another direction. The only option at that point is to throw your automatic response out the window and embrace intentional change.

One exercise I recommend is to *over*stretch your creative boundaries. To travel so far from the norm that you overcome the snap-back to familiar content. It's similar to a vocal exercise. Singers regularly exercise their vocal cords higher than any pitch they will actually hit in a song. They go lower too.

I was noodling on this concept a while back when a thought flew through my head—maybe I could use poetry to describe the journey from traditional content to storytelling. It's a crazy angle that has never been in my wheelhouse—not even close— so it was a perfect exercise to overstretch my boundaries. Here's the result:

> *What shall I do*
> *When the deadline draws near?*
> *Shall I do something new?*
> *Is there something to fear?*

*I hear stories are cool.*
*For me, a frontier.*
*Will I look like a fool*
*If I try it this year?*

*Where shall I start?*
*Is the change too severe?*
*If I lead with the heart*
*Might you all lend an ear?*

*Point one saves a life.*
*Point two makes it clear*
*That conflict and strife*
*Make one want to hear!*

*Turns out there's a way.*
*It seems to appear*
*That stories do pay,*
*Numbers aren't in arrear!*

*If you find this absurd,*
*If you snivel and sneer,*
*Choose a task that's preferred*
*To expand your career.*

Now before you panic, I'm not trying to make you lose your job. I'm also not suggesting you switch from prose to poetry in your marketing content. But I am encouraging you to venture out. It might be time to build new muscles, or to reawaken creative muscles that atrophied long ago. If you're not a fan of poetry you could try writing jokes, or drawing a comic strip, or composing a jingle. Anything outside your comfort zone is fair game.

After all, you have nothing to lose. This is just an exercise. If you aren't able to break free and find a fresh approach, you can always slide back into automatic gear and crank out the tried and true. If you fail the first time, you will live to try something new another day.

## Winding up and moving on

Storytelling is a powerful business tool when applied judiciously. Stories are more memorable than information-packed assets. They reach a broader audience and do a better job of inspiring action. On top of that, they're more likely to grab the attention of C-suite executives.

The question is not so much whether storytelling has business value, but how to adapt storytelling to a corporate context. Novelists don't deal with the push and pull from product managers, keynote executives, legal departments, sales teams, web teams, and content quotas. They don't spin out their content as a story, then turn around and repurpose it as a keynote, infographic, and web copy. They aren't constantly pinging between the highest heights and the deepest depths.

A wholesale transplant of storytelling techniques from the world of novels to the world of business is inadequate and uninformed. Business storytelling requires integral knowledge of the difference between various types of content, as well as the most effective application. In order to hit the target, you must be able to answer the business questions—which tool is most effective for which audience? What type of content will have the biggest impact on brand perception? What content is most effective in converting leads to sales?

The answer is not always "tell a story." Stories have the largest sway on the largest number of people. Stories do for a broad audience what case studies cannot, but there is a flip side to that argument—case studies do for a BDM what stories cannot. The choice is not between a case study and a story, it is between when to use a case study and when to create a story.

Sometimes the wisest answer is to do both. To create an attention-grabbing video story for the highest visibility spots, then write a detailed case study to convert leads to sales. Your sales team will love you for it. Just don't try to turn a case study into a story, because the two don't mix.

If you want to sway impressions, your best bet is to tell a story. But how do you do that? How do you replace a mundane dissemination of stats and metrics with an enduring story? How do you drive storyline development? How do you develop your storytelling skills after years of refining your marketing-speak?

That is the subject of Part 2.

 **Fingertip reminders**

Below is a new way to classify and label content that avoids the nomenclature trap by properly differentiating between type and form.

| | Content Type | | Content Form | | |
|---|---|---|---|---|---|
| | Informational | Inspirational | Written | Video | Graphic |
| **Story** | | X | X | X | |
| **Case Study** | X | | X | X | |
| **Whitepaper** | X | | X | | |
| **eBook** | X | | X | | |
| **Infographic** | X | | | | X |
| **Social media** | X | X | X | X | X |
| **Webinar** | X | | | X | |
| **Blog** | X | (X) | X | | |

## Key Indicators for Informational Content

- Does it answer the questions a potential buyer might ask?
- Is it number-centric?
- Would it be easy to create a Key Learnings list from this content?
- Would it lend itself to an infographic?

## Key Indicators for Inspirational Content

- Would most people care about the topic?
- Would it stir an emotional response?
- Would they be likely to remember it?

And here's a distilled comparison between stories and case studies:

| Stories . . . | Case studies . . . |
|---|---|
| • are about a human experience | • are about a product experience |
| • are inspirational | • are informational |
| • appeal to everyone | • appeal to a narrow, technical audience |
| • are built on a story arc | • are built on a flat, rigid structure |

# PART 2
## LEARN THE MECHANICS

Y OU *CAN* BECOME a better storyteller. Granted, some people have an uncanny knack for uncovering a storyline, some have a natural way with words, and still others have brains that are innately creative. That's okay. We can all learn to be better storytellers.

Besides, we're not looking to win a Pulitzer Prize. I'm not at all sure a Pulitzer Prize winner—or an Academy Award winner for that matter—would excel at business storytelling anyway. There's the whole length constraint, not to mention the maddening battle to get real people and real corporations to join in the fun. Then there's the politics, the legal department, and the crushing demand to feed the content beast.

Still, skills matter and we can work on those. This is not meant to be a course in creative writing, but we will dip our toes into some of the most useful literary techniques to give your stories a bit more punch. We will talk about the basics of video as well. My goal is to leave you with some functional tools to help you refine your craft.

We will talk about creativity too. Compelling stories are more than technically sound—they're also creatively engaging. Those who lean too far one direction or the other don't just miss the bullseye—they might miss the target altogether. Exemplary technique without a bit of genius is dull, while undisciplined creativity is a mess. I like this description by Alice LaPlante.

At one end of the spectrum are those writers who work hard at mastering craft, and turn out exquisitely crafted stories or essays—which are utterly dead and boring. At the other end of the spectrum are the writers who generate exciting and profound initial drafts—but have no control, no way of shaping them into something that can speak to others.[10]

Notice we are not talking about a straight line with "technique" on one end and "creativity" on the other. You do not have to give up some portion of one quality to slide a bit closer to the other. In fact, you *shouldn't* give up one quality for the other. It doesn't work that way.

Choosing between technique and creativity would be absurd, like choosing between milk or cookies. Why on earth would you? You really only get the full effect if you combine the cookies *and* the milk. Preferably whole milk and chewy cookies. *The very best storyteller is both an accomplished wordsmith and a creative spirit.*

One last thing before we get started. It's important that you keep your eye on the proper target, which can be tough when you've spent so many years aiming toward a different bulls-eye. Old habits die hard, so I've crafted a few guidelines to help you find your way.

**Storytelling is never**

- Product-centric
- A regurgitation of messaging
- An obvious sales pitch
- Full of stats and metrics
- Cookie-cutter

**Storytelling is always**

- Human
- Relatable
- Emotive
- Memorable
- Inspiring

And we're off! First up, we will tackle the heart of every story—the storyline.

# THE SINGLE MOST
# IMPORTANT THING

I F I HAD to choose one thing for you to focus on, it would be learning how to craft a good storyline. Start early in the process. Make it part of your selection criteria. Measure every potential story against its storyline, then pick the most compelling option—because if your storyline isn't great, your story won't be either.

Your goal is to fashion a storyline that draws the audience in and holds their attention until the very end. To make a sharp bend right after the setup, trace the arc as high as you possibly can, resolve it in dramatic fashion, and close with a memorable scene.

Aim for the stratosphere. Like this:

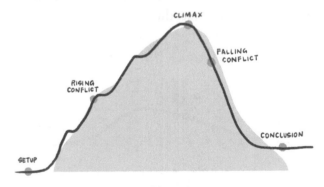

STRATOSPHERE STORY

HUNGER, POVERTY, DISEASE, EDUCATION

Of course, this is business storytelling and the options may be limited. Ideally you are looking for amazing real-life stories enabled by your brand, but those opportunities don't just tumble by every moment of every day. Sometimes you can find them with a lot of sleuthing, but not always. Your topic may be relatable, but nothing that will drive your storyline sky high. Sometimes you have to settle for the mountaintops. That's okay.

Your story arc may look like this:

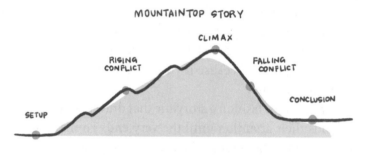

Just make sure there *is* an arc. If you can't hit the stratosphere or the mountaintops, don't settle for the prairie. That's where the mosquitos live. Avoid storylines that simply never gain altitude. They look more like this:

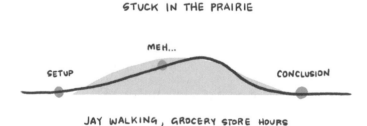

If a barely-there arc is your only option, skip it. Really. Just skip it. Think of something else. Create a different kind of content that you can do well. But don't crank out a "meh" story, because stories *always* influence brand impression—even when you don't want them to.

Your goal as business storyteller is to speak so persuasively that brand perception shifts skyward. On the flip side, a story that leaves the audience unimpressed says exactly that about your brand: unimpressive.

One of the most common mistakes I see is trying to force-fit corporate messaging into the shape of an arc. It won't work. It always lands in the prairie. Improved efficiency, reduced costs, and scalable solutions can't bend a storyline upward. Only a human conflict—not a business challenge—can bend the storyline into an arc. And remember: no arc, no story. So instead of leading with brand messaging, you need to find a unique, touching, human perspective and let the messaging come alive through the story.

## It's not about you

A story is never about you. It's not about your product, your service, or your key messages. *A story is about capturing that moment when your product or service intersects with humanity and changes a life for the better.*

If you don't believe me, perhaps a quantifiable study will help. Thankfully, Professors Adam Grant and Dave Hofmann have already tested the theory at the University of Pennsylvania. Grant and Hofmann zeroed in on the folks who work the phone banks for university fundraising and ran a simple little test. [11]

Like any good test, they measured one thing against another. First, they enlisted the help of two of the university's highest-ranking officials to motivate the fundraising team. The execs dutifully showed up and gave their best pitch. They spoke passionately about their vision for the program. The result? No change in donations.

Next, they enlisted a college student whose life had been changed thanks to receiving a scholarship. Because of donor contributions, the student was able to go to college and even round out their education by studying abroad. It opened doors. It changed a life. The result? Callers were able to raise approximately four times as much money as before. In Grant's words, "the most inspiring way to convey a vision is to outsource it to the people who are actually affected by it."[12]

Get the point? Fundraising isn't about the higher-ups at the university. It's not about the messaging, the programs, or the credentials. Fundraising is about the student who benefited from the scholarship program. In the same way, your story isn't about enlisting the highest-level executives you can possibly wrangle to read a script or supply a quote—it's about finding that person whose life was changed.

That doesn't mean executives don't cast vision. Leaders are absolutely in the vision-casting business! That's what leaders do. Your role is to bring that vision to life. Every story should be anchored by vision. Every hero should be tethered to it. *Storytellers are in the "bringing vision to life" business.*

## The cast

Have you ever read or watched one of those marketing pieces that include a heap of input from a mess of people—but ultimately goes nowhere? You know the type. A round robin of customer employees spouting messaging and proof points willy-nilly—but no storyline. It's just a smorgasbord of sound bites laid end-to-end. The result is rather like content looking for a narrative.

That's the outcome from what I call "the no-plan plan." It typically happens when the main character hasn't been identified and the storyline crafted at the beginning of the process. Instead, we get on the phone—or in front of a camera—and ask a bunch of questions and *then* try to patch something together.

It's sort of like running to Home Depot, buying a bunch of construction materials that look promising, then heading home to figure out what we can possibly make with them. It's too late to impact the design now. We're at the mercy of whatever we threw in the grab bag. Granted, some of the materials might be cool, but are they the very best choice? And some important parts are probably missing, so we have to improvise.

Unfortunately, this scenario is far too common. And the idea that simply gathering information and knocking out a story doesn't work very well can be confusing. I mean, journalists do it all the time, right? They go out, do an interview, and craft an article or video from whatever real-time information is available.

Yes, that's true. It's also true that some of the pieces make the cut and some don't. Some miss critical information. Some have a human interest element and some don't. Some take top billing and some are "also ran." And then it's over. It's on to the next news cycle. Journalists create flash-in-the-pan pieces intended for momentary attention. Yesterday is old news; today is a fresh slate.

That's not your goal. You want to leave a lasting impression that reveals how your brand solves humanity's challenges. You want your content to last, and that will require a different approach. Your role should more closely resemble that of a novelist or screenwriter than a journalist, even though your footprint is considerably smaller. Your goal is to captivate and inspire—not to inform or report—and it takes far more preparation than a run-and-gun approach.

### Who's the main character?

Your first step will be to find someone who has a story worth telling. This is the main character. If you can't find a person whose life was changed by the product or service—you don't have a story. It's that simple, and that important.

In the publishing world the possibilities are limitless. The writer can create any character the mind can imagine—from an authentic character with an amazing life story to a fictional character with superpowers. Alien life and time travel are not out-of-bounds. Writers are free to create a cast of characters and take their story in whatever direction they wish.

Business storytelling is more limited. Corporations are not in the business of writing fiction. We can use personas and scenarios as long as they're grounded in truth—and the legal department is okay with the disclaimers.

Still, nothing beats an authentic human experience. A textbook encounter with a demographically-infused persona can't compare. In business, your best stories are designed around a genuine life journey and carefully built from the ground up. The more personal and emotive the experience, the steeper the bend and the higher the story arc.

Let's assume you have been asked to tell a story about improved vaccine availability in Tanzania. Although I wouldn't turn down the opportunity to talk about the impact of reliable vaccine access to a population desperate for disease management, it wouldn't be my first choice. I would much rather tell the personal story of a mother who faces the future with hope, no longer wondering how many more children she may lose to diphtheria.

Good collective stories have the potential to reach the mountaintops, but it's the individual stories that are stratosphere candidates. Why? Because as humans we relate more to another human than to a population. It's that simple.

So how do you do that? How do you follow a clue and uncover a main character? My advice is to follow what I call the "so what?" trail. Start digging for information, then ask yourself "so what?" at every turn. Why does this information matter? How does it help solve a human problem? And where can I find a personal experience to bring the story to life?

Finding a person with a compelling story can be tricky. Your best bet is to start at the ground floor with a bit of investigative research. Begin with the folks who know the most about the solution: the product manager and product marketer.

The product folks may not have a storytelling frame of mind, but they have the knowledge you need to pull together a storyline. Remember that you have multiple goals. Product information is a must. You can't tell a credible story without it. At the same time, you need to pinpoint a main character and begin to uncover their story. Then you can flesh out the rest of the cast.

The product manager will always tell you how the product works—in as excruciating detail as you are willing to listen. And you can always count on them for a bunch of performance stats. Listen well, because you will need to understand the technical aspects of the solution to tell a plausible story.

Meanwhile, the product marketer will tout features and benefits along with a few phrases from the latest messaging framework thrown in for good measure. Chances are you won't escape without at least a brief review of audience segments, as well as user personas and fictional use cases.

It's best to speak with the product experts right away so you don't go off in some weird direction that is inconsistent with how the solution functions. You also want to capture any differentiating features that might influence how you tell your story. Features and benefits won't capture the spotlight, but you must be true to the product—so grab some time with the product team and start digging.

I suggest you plan your questions ahead of time and follow this basic trajectory:

1.  Learn about the solution
2.  Dig for human impact
3.  Find a personal story

Your challenge won't be to discover the classic marketing metrics and messages. Those will tumble with ease out of the mouths of anyone in the marketing organization. The largest challenge will be to uncover the human impact and identify a main character with a compelling story. Deploying a light tone will help you get there, but it's not enough. You will need to turn your radar on, read past the words, and adjust as you go along.

Here's a fictitious example to help you hone your skills. We will drop into the conversation just as the marketer is winding up their description of the solution:

Product Marketer:    In summary, Product X uses machine learning to provide more targeted and actionable insights. (Notice the marketer made sure to volunteer the lead feature and benefit.)

Storyteller:           Great, thanks. Can you help me understand the human impact?

What difference could this product make to real people in the real world? Can you give me an example?

Product Marketer: Product X can be used to provide better information to doctors at the point of care.

Storyteller: Ah, healthcare is super relevant. Can you identify a specific healthcare problem that Product X might improve?

Product Marketer: Sure. We know that pathologists struggle to make accurate diagnoses because of huge amounts of data and limited time per image set.

Storyteller: Got it. What might that mean to real patients? Can you give me an example?

Product Marketer: Of course. Mammograms read by pathologists alone miss early breast cancer tumors 26% of the time. With Product X, that number drops to 7%.

Storyteller: Whoa, that's huge. How does that translate to patient outcome?

Product Marketer: The earlier a cancer is detected, the greater the chance of survival. When the cancer is caught at its earliest stages—before it has a chance to spread—the 5-year survival rate is 99%. The rate drops to 86% if the cancer has spread to nearby structures or lymph nodes, and once the cancer reaches distant parts of the body the survival rate drops to 27%.

Storyteller: Do you know the human impact in numbers?

Product Marketer: The increase in early detection could save up to 4,800 lives annually in the U.S. alone.

Storyteller: Wow. Do you happen to know a patient story where early detection has made a difference in outcome?

Product Marketer: Absolutely. We have a practice on the East Coast that was one of our earliest adopters. I was speaking with one of the physicians this morning and he told me about Sue. She was a mother with school-age children when Product X was used to help diagnose her breast cancer. They were able to detect her cancer at the earliest stage before it had a chance to spread.

Storyteller: That's amazing. What's Sue's situation now?

Product Marketer: Sue says cancer no longer dominates her life. Although she's sure to get

her regular checkups, she's no longer
preoccupied with being around
to see her children graduate from
high school. As a matter of fact,
she's meeting her oldest daughter
this afternoon to help pick out her
wedding dress! (Queue video b-roll
of wedding dress shopping.)

Notice the evolution of the conversation. We went from
"Product X uses machine learning to provide more targeted
and actionable insights" to "Sue is no longer preoccupied with
being around to see her children graduate from high school."
The Inspirometer just went from a two to a ten.

Never settle for a business problem. Follow the "so what?"
trail wherever it leads until you find the heartbeat of your
story. If your company isn't a storytelling company (yet), you
might encounter some resistance. Perhaps an eye roll or two.
That's okay. Bucking the status quo in order to develop a new
storytelling model is worth a few eye rolls.

And no, it's not always this easy to find a story—but
I've had it happen just this way. Other times you may need
to beg for an introduction to the physician and speak with
them directly. Paint the picture. Get them onboard. Or the
marketer might refer you to another team member who
knows of a good story. Or someone on the sales team could
know one. Your job is to unearth more and more potential
contacts until you find a main character with a compelling
story.

Don't be afraid to keep digging. If you're a B2B company,
the stories you are looking for probably live in your customer's
customer base, not yours—like the physician who identified
Sue. If you take the right approach, asking for your customer's

help needn't be a giant one-sided favor; it's an opportunity for them to be part of the story.

Regardless of the route, I have found that the story unfolds pretty quickly once the correct person is on the phone. You just have to put in the effort to find a good contact—and the next, and the next—and convince them to speak with you. Once you find the right person, it can be exhilarating to hear a tale of human triumph tumble from their mouth. Finally—after all your hard work—you've hit the jackpot.

Meanwhile, don't be surprised if you hear the word "impossible" a few times along the way. That's routine. I have circumvented internal naysayers for every meaningful story I have ever produced. Once you land a few stories, you can use them as examples to help bring others along. Some folks will capture the vision easily; others might have trouble leaving the comfort of a familiar style. If your company is counting on you to be a storyteller, you need to find a way to navigate those hurdles.

When you hit the inevitable roadblock, search for another route. I would encourage you to trust your nose. If you feel there might be a good story around the next bend—or the next, or the next—keep digging. True storytelling is not for the faint of heart, but it's worth the struggle. Business storytelling, despite the abundance of conversation, is still a frontier. Pioneers don't give up easily.

Now let's examine Sue's story a little closer. She's an ordinary person in a tough circumstance. Cancer can happen to anyone. And she cares about how her illness might impact her children. Most any parent would feel the same. She could, in effect, be any of us—yet she faces an unwanted and arduous journey. And she survives. Sue is ordinary and yet extraordinary. She is relatable and yet her perseverance and grace make her inspirational.

Now granted, this is a business story. We don't want to lose sight of the solution in favor of puppies and rainbows, but if we do our job right we don't have to. Instead, we will credit Product X with the outcome, but we are going to tuck the product specifics *underneath* the overarching change in Sue's life and that of her family. Product X is now saving lives, which is far more captivating, inspirational, and memorable than a device that uses machine learning to improve insights.

So now we have a main character. Our story will focus on Sue. The story arc will trace her story and credit the product with the outcome. Now let's fill out the rest of the cast.

### What about the hero?

So is Sue the hero of the story? Not really. Often the main character and the hero are one and the same—think Frodo Baggins, Luke Skywalker, or Harry Potter—but they aren't always. They certainly aren't in this case. Sue's role is nothing like the hero part. Frodo destroyed the ring, Luke battled the evil empire, and Harry slayed Voldemort, but Sue is not in the business of saving the day. She needs someone else to be her hero.

So are you the hero? Nope, that's not your role either. Not in this case anyway. You didn't order the x-ray or insist on the very best lab technology. Sue's hero is the physician. This is the person who encouraged Sue to stay on top of her preventative care and enlisted a service that uses the very best method for early detection. The physician can speak of your product's contribution to Sue's early diagnosis and how that influenced her outcome. The physician is data-driven, tech-savvy, and outcome-centric, but above all, they care that Sue is alive to watch her children grow. And they can vouch for the value of your product or service. The physician is the hero of the story.

Which brings up another point—marketing's use of the word "hero" can be confusing. We often use "hero" to mean prominent. Bigger than life. A hero image is the biggest and baddest banner image at the top of a webpage or article. It fills the most high-profile location and typically takes up the full width of the page. A hero image is the most visible and has the loudest voice.

Forget that definition when it comes to storytelling. The hero is not always the most visible or the loudest. They *might* be bigger than life, but they might not. The hero is the advocate who works tirelessly to save the day. The champion of a cause. They make sure the main character gets home safely. Or accomplishes a dream. Or is cured of cancer.

Now let's step back a minute and examine the hero role based on your business model. If you sell to other businesses, chances are you will never get to play the hero. You simply don't have a direct link to the main character. You can't swoop in and save their day—you don't even know where they live. Your customer will play that part.

However—and this is an important however—if you're one of those companies that sells directly to consumers, you do get to play hero. It's a sweet job. But for now, let's assume you work in a business-to-business (B2B) or business-to-business-to-consumer (B2B2C) model. No hero status for you.

### Where do you fit in?

Okay, so now it might seem like all of the good parts are taken. Sue is the main character and the customer is the hero. Dang, where does that leave us? Comic sidekick?

Thankfully, no. Your job—in storytelling lingo—is to be the mentor. To figure out what a mentor does, let's take another peek at Frodo's dilemma. It's his quest, but he couldn't have done it without Gandalf. Gandalf arranged, supported, and defended Frodo and the entire cast of supporting characters throughout the journey. He brings the wisdom and power that propels Frodo to success. He will do anything to help the cause—even die (temporarily, of course).

Your role is to be the Gandalf to Frodo's crusade. The Yoda that prepares Luke for battle. The Dumbledore who guides and teaches Harry. The story can't succeed without you, because *you are the one who equips the hero to save the day.*

One quick note—don't settle for being a sidekick. You are not Samwise Gamgee, R2D2, or Ronald Weasley. There's no element of lesser than. Certainly not of bumbling. Instead, you serve a unique and powerful role. You fill in every gap so that the hero can save the day.

So basically—you're a big deal. The very image of a mentor implies wisdom and power. Your role is to supply the knowledge and tools necessary for success, but you're not an attention-seeker. Your job is not to steal the spotlight—your job is to direct the spotlight toward the main character as you're sliding proverbial weapons into the hands of the hero.

### Can I just skip Sue?

It's tempting—and way too common—to tell the story without Sue. It's certainly easier. If you ditch Sue, everything becomes simpler. The only phone interview you need to arrange is with your customer. You know how to do that. The only legal release you need is from the physician along with a sign-off from their practice. Not bad at all. Just don't confuse that type of content with a story. No changed life? No story.

If you're working on a video—and without Sue it may not be worth the resources—the production can get a little tricky because of the healthcare industry. It's highly regulated, privacy sensitive, and reputation conscious.

Even without Sue, physicians won't want you roaming the halls with a camera as long as there are patients in the building. You will need to arrange off-hours access to the doctor's office. Then you will need a video release form for every person who is visually identifiable or has anything to say. And you may want to supplement with paid talent to play the part of those patients you're avoiding, so you will need video releases from them too.

Now let's throw Sue into the mix. Things just got way more complicated. First, the physician might flat-out refuse to identify a patient. They will certainly insist on speaking with them first before giving you any contact information. And physicians are *always* busy. It's a pretty big request for them to identify potential patients and call down the list until they find someone to sign on. You might not be able to clear that hurdle.

Assuming you win the battle, you will also need to conduct a phone interview with the patient before you can craft the storyline. Then you will need a HIPAA release from the patient, and there's a good chance the physician practice will want you to do double-duty and have the patient sign their version for their own files.

Then the video releases expand a good bit. You will want to capture Sue within the context of her life and family, so that probably means you will need video releases from Sue's husband, children, and anyone else in her close circle. Maybe even her best friend from work.

Those releases might be tricky because individuals can be shy about appearing in a commercial video. It can also get awkward when everyone who signs a release form expects to speak in the video. On top of that, you have another location to shoot, which entails at least one more shoot day and probably another travel day. The timeline is going to extend. The workload will go up. So will the cost. Do you see how much more complicated it is to tell Sue's story? So why not skip Sue and run with a generic customer testimonial? Because it's *so* worth the extra effort. Sue's story *is* the story. I have found it's better to fight for one story about Sue than ten generic "the doctor likes our product" pieces. When Sue shares her deep concerns about her children, the audience can feel it. "I was so scared. I didn't want to leave my children without a mother," wields way more power than, "patients are often concerned about the impact to their family."

Sue is your version of the scholarship recipient. She is the reason why people will listen to your story. She has more influence than you do. She even has more influence than your customer does. Sue is the "so what?" part of your story. She gives the audience a reason to care.

### Characters by business model

The scenario we just explored works beautifully for a B2B2C model, but not all companies operate that way. Some are closer to the consumer and others are further away. Understanding where the consumer, or some other representation of humanity, fits in to the picture is paramount to storyline development. Every business eventually impacts people—you just have to figure out how. Keep your eye on the human element and you will be able to find a workable approach, regardless of the business model.

Let's look at a model that can be difficult to connect to a human problem—business to business (B2B). These companies specialize in products or services that help other businesses run smoothly. Perhaps they specialize in small business loans. Or rent office space. Maybe they provide software analytics. Or supply chain management. There are tons of products and services that don't directly touch consumers. So how do you carve out a personal story when the solution seems so impersonal?

Let's start by revisiting the case study from ScreaminFastData™—the company that delivered a secure cloud platform to process electronic payments for retailers. If we dig a little deeper, we might be able to figure out a storyline.

As a reminder, here's the case study outline:

- Background:
  - › Consumers are increasingly shopping online and making mobile payments.
  - › Globally, the mobile payment market is approaching $2.1 trillion.
  - › Credit card fraud exceeds $30 billion globally and is expected to double in 10 years.
  - › SmokinFastPay™ is the largest payment processing provider in the world.

- Problem:
  - › Consumers demand speed and security for their payments, whether in person, online, or using a smartphone.

- Solution:
  - › SmokinFastPay deployed a revolutionary new cloud-based data platform by ScreaminFastData.

- Results:
  - › Transaction speeds improved by 23%.
  - › Security breaches decreased by 69%.

- Conclusion:

  > ScreaminFastData solved SmokinFastPay's
    business problem (and it can solve yours too).

To figure out the storyline, you always start in the same place—with the "so what?" questions. Let's say you've already spoken with the product manager and the product marketer. You've learned a lot. You understand the technology and its ability to reduce processing speed and improve security, but there's no Sue to be found.

Now you speak with the customer. The CIO tells you the same thing—processing speed and data security are a big deal. And they speak about their appreciation for the analytics and load balancing. All good information, and all from their point of view. Your challenge will be to shift to a human point of view.

Here's the new information you learned from the customer:

- They like the service because *their* customers—the retailers—can clear payments for more customers faster, which improves their bottom line.

  > (As an individual, I'm not super interested in the retailer's bottom line.)

- It's less expensive to give retailers top-level security because it's all included in the platform.

  > (*Again* with the corporate bottom line. Clearly not a human topic.)

- The platform includes real-time analytics, which improves service and reduces in-house development cost.

> ➤ (Corporate cost is not something the general populace cares about.)

- It also includes the ability to load balance nodes and quickly redirect to secondaries.

  > ➤ (Whew, now I *really* don't care. I don't even know what that means.)

Now let's think "story" instead of "case study." The corporate bottom line isn't a life-changer for any of us. We need a topic that is relevant to a lot of people. Remember, here is our target:

*A story is about capturing that moment when your product or service intersects with humanity and changes a life for the better.*

Yikes. How are we going to come up with a storyline? Let's start by pulling together those pieces that might be relevant to an individual.

- Credit card fraud exceeds $30 billion globally and is expected to double in 10 years.
- The solution decreases security breaches by 69%.
- It also improves transaction speeds by 23%.

Credit card fraud is definitely on the "stuff a lot of people care about" list. We all care when someone steals our card information and takes a shopping trip on our dime, even if the charges are reversed by the bank. It's not just about the money—it's about the hassle and the unwanted encroachment into our personal lives.

Most people have received the dreaded "call your credit card company" text. The last time it happened to me, I was flurrying around my hotel room in British Columbia, cramming the last few errant items into my suitcase before check-out.

I called. And I found out that while I was packing, my credit card was busily making purchases at gas stations and shopping malls across Nebraska, Kansas, and Texas. I looked in my wallet. Yup, my credit card was still there. Skimmers are the worst. If a solution could decrease my chances of a repeat performance by 69%, I'd be a fan.

Another annoying feature of the consumer experience is waiting in line. I realize I was supposed to master the art in Kindergarten, but I still don't like it. Most people don't, and the slower the line, the higher the frustration. And it leaves a bad impression, which is never good for a retailer.

So would credit card fraud work as a lede with transaction speed as a secondary topic? It might if we tell it from a human point of view, but how do we do that? We don't have a direct connection to the consumer. Our customer doesn't even interface with the consumer. We are too far removed from the human experience to expect to find a real-life story.

So what should we do? Simple. Find another way to show the human impact of credit card fraud. A real-life story has power, but every story doesn't have to be a real-life reenactment as long as the scenario *could* be real. And no, I'm not talking about a generic marketing persona and scenario story. You need to find a highly relatable, human perspective.

Here are a few quick ideas. Any of these concepts or a hundred others could make a great video.

- A couple on their honeymoon finds their credit card won't work when they check in at the hotel.

- A nervous adventurer is about to tackle Mount Everest with a mountain of gear. Meanwhile, her

Sherpa guide receives a note from the credit card company: "retain and destroy card."

- A dad buying pizza for the little league team after their big win has his payment declined.

Throw in some exasperatingly long lines and you have a winner. Everyone will be able to relate. And, of course, you can still credit the customer as the hero and take your subtle bow as the mentor. The only difference is that you have hired someone to play the main character. It's not a real-life story, but it could be.

### The more the merrier?

Characters are good, right? So more is better? No, absolutely not. The audience will most likely be struggling to fit your story into their over-packed workday. They have back-to-back meetings, so reading or watching your story is not a leisurely activity for them. A consumable story demands that you pick just the right content and pack it tight. Your target footprint might be six minutes of reading time or three minutes of video. So make it count. Dredging up everyone from Sue's next door neighbor to her cousin Eddie won't help you. It's a distraction.

The same is true with the customer. You don't need the CEO, the CIO, the plant manager, and the technician to all pipe in with their two cents. The audience has to mentally process and integrate every character you add. It leaves them spending brain cycles trying to catch up rather than follow along in the story.

If the severe restriction on cast size is confusing, I get it. This is another one of those situations where business storytelling does not mimic the publishing world. A novelist has 200 pages or more to tell their story. A screenwriter has at least 90 minutes. They have the time and space to flesh out the relational web with a myriad of family, friends, coworkers, acquaintances, and enemies. Maybe even a few pets. The publishing world can devote whatever time is necessary to develop each character so that the audience isn't left filling in the blanks.

You don't have that kind of time and space. You need to develop each character just enough to disclose their identity and spin them into the story—so you take a different approach. Your cast of characters needs to be short and buttoned up. I suggest you use one voice for the main character, one voice for your superhero customer, and one voice to tell how your product equipped the hero to save the consumer's day. If you're telling a B2C story, you're down to two voices to represent two characters. That's it.

So what do you do with the orbital characters? The ones whose lives revolve around Sue and her battle for health? Good storytelling demands that you round out your characters, but time and space are severely limited. So how do you capture the heartbreak of Sue's husband? The fear in the hearts of her children?

Let's talk video for a minute. Harsh as it may sound, hubby doesn't get to talk. Neither do the kids. They appear visually but not audibly. *The audience will experience Sue's story—and her family's—through Sue's voice.* She can speak of her husband's pain while you capture b-roll of the couple having a heart-to-heart. Maybe a consoling hug on the back deck. She can tell of her children's fears while you capture touching images of Sue with her children. For a written piece you take the same approach and include professional photos. You can tell a more connected story—one that doesn't make the audience play mental catch up—if you let Sue tell it. She can capture the complex emotions and relationships without adding more voices.

The same is true for your customer. Let's say you arranged for the CEO to speak on video in an interview style. Chances are your subject will have plenty of video experience and won't be a nervous mess, although anything is possible. The bigger risk is an overly formal delivery with lots of company flag-waving and industry lingo. They may also need help to illustrate exactly how your product or service fits into the story. You're going to have to find a smooth way to feed them the details so they can voice it in their own words—without adding more voices.

The key is cohesion. You want to keep the storyline tight. With such a small footprint, every second counts. It's your job to keep each character on point in order to keep the storyline intensely focused. Each of the primary characters will voice their perspective and that of the secondary characters that surround them—always with an eye toward Sue's experience. Visuals will bring the story to life.

So how do you pull that off? How do you keep the human element center stage while attributing the life-changing outcome to your brand? How do you create a compelling personal story—possibly with a technical angle—and tell it with a limited cast?

## Give it to me step-by-step

The trick to producing a well-developed story with a limited cast is to work from a detailed plan. Your plan should be intentional, thorough, and creative. More than a loose guideline. It should be exact enough to trace the story arc, yet flexible enough to accommodate on-set realities.

Let's start by looking at a traditional approach to content development. The process typically goes something like this:

1. Conduct research
2. Identify key points
3. Write article or shoot video
4. Review and polish
5. Publish

I have oversimplified the process, but that is the basic order. What might appear as a "seat of your pants" approach is more likely born of repetition—and it works most of the time. After all, most of our marketing content is informative and fits into an existing mold: case study, white paper, eBook, web copy, social media, webinar, podcast, blog. Those pieces are predictable. We can afford to insert blank paper and follow an old game plan.

Storytelling requires a more thorough process, particularly on the front end—*before* the writing or filming. It looks more like this:

- Conduct *exploratory* research
- Identify *a human conflict, cast of characters,* and key points
- *Conduct targeted research*
- *Design detailed plan*
- Write article or shoot video
- Review and polish
- Publish

## Exploratory research

It's important to recognize that storytelling has a two-phased approach toward research rather than a single pass. The exploratory phase casts a wide net and will test your sleuthing skills. It has a lot of similarities to a sales funnel—you are digging for leads and qualifying potential winners.

You may find yourself doing a *lot* of digging. Start internally. Speak with the product manager and product marketer—multiple times if needed. Get to know the sales team and ask for their help. Track down new leads. One time I found an amazing story from a person who sat across the table from me at a corporate dinner.

Then reach out to your customers. Get their perspective. Ask to speak with your customer's customers. Explain the opportunity, make them comfortable, and get them on board. If you reach a dead end, circle back internally and ask for more information and more leads. Your initial research should lead you to a willing main character with a compelling story.

## Conflict, cast, and key points

Once you have identified a main character, put words around their conflict, ferret out the rest of the cast, and summarize the key points. Write it down. Put it in a deck. Figure out who needs to buy in and get their blessing. It's important to get concept approval now, because this will be the kernel of your story. That doesn't mean that you ask everyone for their input—you may never get a story published that way. But *someone* needs to be on your team who can help advocate for the story.

### Targeted research

Now that you have committed to the heartbeat for your story, it's time to learn more. You have probably already spoken with your main character once to gauge their interest. Now it's time to speak with them again.

Pick up the phone. Once you get them on the line, remember you are not working on traditional content development. Your typical corporate communication strategy is no longer adequate. Instead, you must continue to protect your company's interests while adopting a more personal tone.

This is not a corporate-to-corporate conversation—it's a human-to-human conversation. Break the ice. Make them comfortable with the process. Then figure out what makes them tick. Learn their passions and their priorities. This is where you will uncover a novel approach for your story. It's also where you make them comfortable enough to sign a release form.

Then get back in touch with your customer. The first pass was to chat about options and to measure interest. This time you're looking for details and formal commitment. When you speak with them, don't just speak with the CEO—speak with the CIO, the program manager, and anyone else who can help you flesh out the story and fill in the blanks.

By the time you complete your targeted research, you should know the story better than anyone else on the planet. You understand what the product can and can't do, the capabilities your customer leaned on to create the result, and the life-changing experience of your main character.

### Detailed plan

Now grow that kernel into a detailed plan. This is a key differentiator between an informative piece and an inspirational piece. Flesh it out. Be creative. How will you create an opening that attracts attention? Compel your audience to stick with you through twists and turns until the final close? Where are the human touch points? How do they relate to the product? And how do you weave in main points without destroying the human connection? This is the foundation for your story. The outline of your story arc.

For a literary piece you can use a solid outline—the kind your teacher made you create in English class. It should have a header for each section, and bullet points underneath describing the main points.

For video, you will need a more elaborate format. Video production is more complex than a written piece for at least two reasons: the production team is larger, and the visual elements are an integral part of the story. You need a planning mechanism to tie together the script, visuals, and key points so they all work in harmony.

Through the years, I've come up with a simple four-column format that I create together with a top-notch video team. I typically take the lead on the early end of the process in order to find the main character, uncover the human conflict, define the key points, and gather tons of personal tidbits to add color to the story.

Then I go to the video team and share the basic building blocks. We talk about the main character and their journey, the human connection, and the role of the customer and the product. Then the director takes first pass at fleshing out the creative and flowing it into a detailed plan. We ping it back and forth, adjusting and refining until it's perfect.

Here's what the first two scenes might look like for Sue's story:

| VISUALS | STORYLINE | KEY POINTS |
|---|---|---|
| 1 | We open on a close-up profile of Sue in her garden. She's planting. It's a quiet morning— peaceful and calm. There are pots of flowers and flats of seedlings in the background. We see her study the flower bed, carefully considering where to place each plant. We see her on her knees, hand on the small shovel as she slowly digs in the dirt. She does not wear gloves. We watch her face, deep in thought as she places a plant in the hole, draws the dirt around the base, and pats it firmly into place. The shots are intimate and deeply focused, revealing little about the surroundings but instead drawing the audience into her inner narrative. | **Opening – we meet Sue and get to know her.** *VO- (Sue): Talking about her pre-diagnosis life and the elements that matter to her most— her husband and children, her work at the Children's Hospital, and gardening. We establish Sue's strength and how much her family depends on her. We hear how she moved her father into her own home and cared for him after his fall from a ladder, all while continuing to work and care for her family. And we subtly capture her joy—Sue is a happy person and she loves life.* | • Intro Sue<br>• Her strength and deep love of family<br>• Gardening, a glimpse of beauty and renewal<br>• Love of life |

| | VISUALS | STORYLINE | KEY POINTS |
|---|---|---|---|
| 2 | Intimate scene of Sue and her husband Henry together. She walks into the house with dirty hands and goes straight to the kitchen sink, where she places soap on her hands and begins to wash. Henry is making coffee. Sue puts more soap on her hands and scrubs away the last of the dirt as Henry pours two cups of coffee and sets them on the table. The two sit down, talking and spending time together. We capture the intimacy of their connection— subtle glances across the table, the moment he reaches over and grazes her hand. We see photos of her children in the background.<br><br>Cut to after school, we see her girls burst onto the scene, laughing and talking. They have just gotten off the school bus. | **Conflict – we show the confusing path of cancer diagnosis and treatment.** VO- *(Sue): Talking about the devastation of her diagnosis. The childhood memories of her mother's death from the same disease. Her desire to shield her husband and children, yet knowing that she can't. Wanting to be there for her girls as they grow up— graduation, wedding, etc. Feeling a sense of loss, yet hopeful for recovery.* | • Understanding the struggle that Sue (and many other women) face with a breast cancer diagnosis<br><br>• Introducing the genetic component, the loss of her mother, and her desire to protect her own children<br><br>• Overriding theme of hope and strength during adversity |

This level of preparation may seem like overkill, but it's not. Not if you're going to tell a stand-out story. This is the document that will map out every scene, inform every interview, dictate the movements of any paid talent, and drive production decisions from beginning to end. You can come up with your own template that works best for you, but don't slight the preplanning. Without it your story may drift and you will lose some of your creative options.

Here's an example. I was on an introductory phone call with the main character for a new video, trying to learn about his journey and find an angle for the story. I asked him to tell me about himself—what mattered to him most and what he loved to do. His answer was straightforward. What mattered to him most was providing for his family, and what he loved to do was fish. He had lost both during the deepest part of his struggle. Now, thanks to Product X, he was back to work and back on the lake.

Here was a story. A life's journey through loss and recovery. But how could we capture it on video? The family dynamic was easy, but the fishing scenes were critical. This is how we could visually illustrate his path from wholeness, to adversity, to renewal. A second chance at life.

Without extensive preplanning, we would have lost the opportunity. The video shoot was in late fall, long after most of the local lakes were closed for fishing. The weather was iffy, the production schedule was tight, we needed fishing licenses for part of the crew, and we had to find an open lake within a short driving distance. It took two weeks of web searches and phone calls to find a location—two weeks we wouldn't have had if we'd waited until shoot time to fill in the details. On-site adjustments are always part of the process, but showing up ill-prepared is an option killer.

You can also use your planning document to design the

interview questions. The main character will be telling their personal story, so all you have to do is keep it authentic and make sure to hit all the main points. The customer is more likely to come to the interview with ready-made answers in their head, so I find it helpful to insert notes within the questionnaire and share them ahead of time—here is the question, here is the type of answer we are looking for. If they forget a main point during the video shoot, just give them a quick reminder and roll the camera again. Whatever you do, don't feed them a script. Let them tell it in their own words. There is an appropriate time for scripting, but a heartfelt personal story isn't it.

### Draft, Polish, and Publish

The hardest part is over. Once you have a firm plan, the remaining steps are straightforward: write the article or shoot the video; review and polish; publish. The execution will be easier and the story will be better because you did your homework ahead of time.

Before we move on, we need to talk about the relative weight of the characters. You will need to consider the level of each character's input. How do you balance the voices so the human story shines through, yet the customer gets to be the hero and your brand is recognized as the mentor?

## Keeping it all in balance

The main character is the central figure in the story and your primary connection to the audience, so be sure to give them adequate time and space. I typically give the main character at least 50% of the weight. The hero and the mentor share the remaining space, with the hero having the larger portion. If there are only two characters, you can give the main character a larger platform. It looks something like this, although the relative weights are not etched in stone.

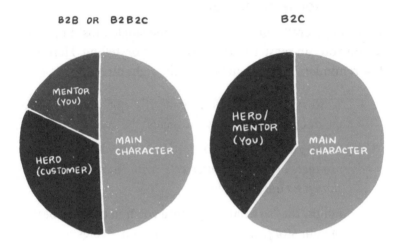

It's not my intent to make storyline design appear formulaic. It's not. This is just a guideline to help you balance your story so it remains human.

In this section, we talked about how to find the heartbeat of your story, design a storyline, and execute it with precision. In the next section, we'll cover a few tools to help you develop your storytelling skills. Some elements of storytelling are universal, some are specific to prose, and some are unique to video. Before we hit those topics, here are some reminders to help you craft a great storyline.

**Fingertip reminders**

Learning to craft a great storyline is the single most important lesson you can master to improve your storytelling. Here are a few reminders to help you head in the right direction.

- A story is never about you. It's not about your product, service, or key messages.

- *A story is about capturing that moment when your product or service intersects with humanity and changes a life for the better.*

- Follow the "so what?" trail until you find the heartbeat of your story, and then fill out the other roles.

  > The main character is the person whose life is changed.

  > The hero is the advocate who works tirelessly to change the life of the main character. Often this is your customer. If you sell directly to consumers, this may be you.

  > The mentor equips the hero to save the day. This is the person who supplies the knowledge and tools necessary for success. If you sell to other businesses, this is your role.

- Storytelling requires a thorough process.

  1. Conduct ***exploratory research***

  2. Identify ***a human conflict, cast of characters***, and key points

  3. Conduct ***targeted research***

4. Design *detailed plan*

5. Write article or shoot video

6. Review and polish

7. Publish

- Use any format you like to create a detailed plan. For an article, that might be a simple outline that traces the story arc. For a video, you also need to map the storyline to the visuals.

- Here's a simple template I often use:

| | VISUALS | STORYLINE | KEY POINTS |
|---|---|---|---|
| 1 | *Fill this column with a description of every scene you plan to capture and every person you plan to show: the main character with their family, b-roll of a town, interview footage, etc.* | Fill this column with the story you're trying to tell: the background, the conflict, the resolution, including whose voice will be heard. | *Fill this column with the key points you're trying to hit. This keeps you on track while filming so nothing gets left out.* |

I typically give the main character at least 50% of the weight in a story. The hero and the mentor share the remaining space, but none of these are etched in stone.

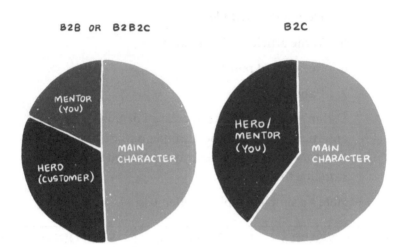

# TOOLS OF THE TRADE

S TORYTELLING IS AN art, but that doesn't mean it's a fly-by-the-seat-of-your-pants adventure. Learning the time-honored techniques of a craft isn't confining; it's liberating. Artists go to school. They study. They pick up new tools, learn new techniques, and build new skills. And they get better.

Storytelling is the same. Every author will eventually find their unique voice, but the good ones also know the tools of the trade. We will start with a few universal tools you can use regardless of whether you're creating a written piece or a video.

## Use a measuring stick

*"At the end of the day people won't remember what you said . . . they will remember how you made them feel."*

—Maya Angelou

The human-to-human connection is a defining point in storytelling—one which separates it from traditional content. But how do you get there? How do you know if you are on the right path? And how can you make your story the very best that it can be?

I keep a checklist of good storytelling characteristics and measure my story against it. Sort of like a measuring stick. I use it at the beginning when I'm searching for a storyline, in the middle as I'm fleshing out the details, and all the way through the final polish. I measure against a smorgasbord of enticing qualities and try to make sure my story encompasses all of them.

The list isn't fancy. It's not particularly eloquent. It's not even comprehensive—a list of good storytelling qualities could go on and on—yet it's simple enough to be helpful and hits the main points. It reminds me where I am going and keeps me on track.

Here is the checklist I look for in every business story I create.

### High-impact

Remember the Impact Quadrant? It's time to use it. The Impact Quadrant will help you gauge whether a story is worth telling or not. It's especially helpful during the germination phase to help you pinpoint the very best topic.

Aim for six or higher on *both* the Interest and Intensity scales—the top right quadrant. That's where the great stories live.

## IMPACT QUADRANT

If you're not sure how many people might be interested in the topic, ask yourself a few questions:

- Would my family or neighbors care?
- Is it cross-generational?
- Does it reach across economic or geographic boundaries?

And here's a list of questions to help you measure intensity:

- Will the topic evoke a passionate response?

- Does it have a cult following?

- Is it intensely important to a geographical area or vocation?

- Does it have a strong generational history? How about gender?

Before we move on, let's dig a bit deeper into the quadrants. Here's a summary that might help:

- Top-right – These are your storytelling winners. Everybody cares about your topic and they care a lot.

- Top-left – This quadrant can be confusing, particularly if the topic is related to your product wheelhouse. These are your people. They care about the same things you care about. Still, the topic lacks broad appeal. It can't bend the story arc dramatically upward. This quadrant makes for great informational content, but it won't make a good story.

- Bottom-right – Skip it. There's not enough passion about this topic to make it worth your while.

- Bottom-left – The complete duds.

Now that you have a definitive method for choosing which stories to tell, let's see what other qualities you can use to see how your story measures up.

### Compelling characters

It's worth the extra effort to find a bang-up cast. It might seem that the plot alone will carry the story, but it won't. Your choice of characters can either bring the story to life—or bury it. Even a few seconds of verbal stumbling or the dreaded deer-in-headlights look can tank a video.

If you're lucky enough to have multiple options for a main character, choose the one with the raspy voice and sparkly eyes. Find the person who reveals their deepest joys and fears. The one that cries easily and laughs even easier. Skip the character with the monotone voice and placid countenance. And make sure your hero is interesting too. Humdrum characters make for a humdrum story.

### Engaging

We've all read a boring textbook. Even if you're interested in the topic, the style and length can make anyone nod off. Odds are you will abandon that book in favor of something more engaging. It's simply too much of a slog to get through.

Your literary or video style matters. A lot. If your style is overly formal, or detailed, or verbose, your content will be the same. Instead, figure out how to make your content appealing. Spend time dissecting your storyline to find ways to draw the audience in. Is there a poignant visual image? Do you need to vary the length of your sentences? Adjust your vocabulary? Tweak the pacing in your video? How about changing the music? It will be worth your while to fight for an engaging style.

### Captivating

Once you have engaged the audience, figure out how to hold on to them. What can you do to make them enjoy the journey from beginning to end? They need to be itching to turn the page, or to see the next scene unfold. Analyze your story repeatedly for any spots that drag, then either take them out or change them.

The middle of a story is prime exit ramp territory. This is where you might be tempted to throw in too many product details or key messages. Don't do it. Reveal just enough product information to support the storyline and skip the messaging. If it's not integral to the life-changing outcome, this isn't the place. Instead, save all those features, benefits, stats, and messages for a case study. Or a blog. Or whitepaper. Whatever you do, don't give your audience an invitation to exit.

### Surprising

You don't need a huge surprise ending, but be sure to play up the little twists and turns along the way. Most stories have them. An unexpected stumble on the way to work reveals an underlying health issue. An unreliable generator in a rural area stops kids from learning on a computer. Accumulated dirt on solar panels reduces power output to a remote outpost.

Keep your eye out for surprises and weave them into the story. You can use them for a number of reasons. Perhaps you want to add a bit of suspense, provide a dose of relief, or reveal a new character quality. Just don't overplay your hand. Have you ever read or watched a story and knew exactly what the "twist" would be before the author got there? Predictable is not one of the characteristics we're going for. Still, genuine twists and turns along the way can make your story interesting.

## *Memorable*

A good story leaves the audience wanting more. It tumbles around in their brain and finds its way into their thoughts. It's unforgettable. Like a good book or movie that pops up in conversations years later—the ones that hatch memes and spur hopes for a sequel.

While your business story may not—and probably will not—achieve that level of acclaim, it's still a good quality to keep front-and-center. Your story should make enough of a mark for others to talk about it. You want them to share the link, bring it up in sales calls, and remember it at next year's event. Ideally, it will set a new benchmark in your marketing organization.

## *Inspiring*

Yet in the end, memorable isn't enough. After all, your goal is not to entertain—your goal is to inspire the audience to action.

We tell business stories for one reason—to gain more business. Have you changed brand impression? Gotten the attention of your C-suite customer base? Opened the doors for your sales team?

In a nutshell, is your audience motivated to action? Are they compelled to pick up the phone—or at least answer it—to talk about a new partnership? Do they ask questions? Bring new ideas to the table? Does it lead to new ventures? If so, you have inspired your audience and made a mark in the storytelling world.

Okay, so you have a checklist of great storytelling qualities to measure against. Now let's talk about some steps you can take to help you get there. This is not meant to be an exhaustive list, nor will it assure you of a new career as a creative writer or filmmaker—but it will help you take your business storytelling to the next level.

## Establish the tone

One thing you should settle on early in the process is the tone. The tone encapsulates the predominant emotion across the entire piece. A single scene might show the main character at a low point—tired, scared, or anxious—yet the overall tone of the piece may be hopeful. Tone defines the emotion that wins out. Think of it as the overarching mood. Will your story be uplifting or melancholy? Sensitive or tough? Serious or humorous?

Remember Sue, the breast cancer survivor? Below are a couple of ways we could approach her story. It's your job to figure out which tone fits Sue better—and which one will ultimately make the greatest impression.

| Option 1 | Option 2 |
|---|---|
| Soft yet strong, nervous yet hopeful. Ultimately uplifting. | Teary, sensitive, and vulnerable. Ultimately restorative. |

The choice you make will dramatically influence the story. In either case the solution will ultimately provide the tools for victory, but the emotive journey will follow different routes and the final takeaway will land in a different emotional space. In the first story Sue is a pillar of strength. In the second she's sensitive and fragile.

Once you decide on the tone, write it on the top of the written outline or video plan. Keep it front and center. Use it to inform everything from the interview questions to the storyline to the video scenes and shot design.

Regardless of the path you choose, a story isn't worth much if no one consumes it. So how do you draw the audience into your story? How do you keep them invested in the outcome until you release them after the final scene? We'll tackle that challenge next.

## Spread the glue

It's not enough to find a good storyline, pack it with compelling characters, and settle on the tone. You also have to find a way to form and maintain a bond with the audience. You can think of it as applying a little glue during the opening moments of the story and spreading it along the entire story arc until the final curtain. A journey without exit ramps.

### Emotive opener

Have you ever attended a concert that had the audience on their feet from the first chord to the last? That's not happenstance, and it's not based solely on the quality of the music. A band that knows how to rock a stadium is intentional about creating their playlist. They never start with an unknown song from their latest album. Instead, the opener is always a crowd-pleaser—a song that exploits the intimate connection between the audience and the music.

You need to do the same thing with your story—work to form an emotive connection with the audience up-front. People relate to the ups and downs of the human experience, so lead with that. If you don't, you'll lose them right out of the chute. Here's an illustration: about 20% of people who start watching a YouTube video will bail out after the first 10 seconds.[13] The same effect is true for a written piece.

You need to nail that intro by hitting on the heart of the story. One of these options might work for Sue:

- Losing a parent is devastating for a child.
- I never thought it would happen to me.
- Gardening always soothes my mind. It gives me a break from the worry.

On the other hand, leading with information is a pretty predictable yawn-inducer—one you may not recover from. I would advise against this type of opening:

- Dr. Wilguns works at Eseley Hospital in Shiny Rock, Vermont.
- Eseley Hospital in Shiny Rock, Vermont, was looking for a way to reduce turnaround time for pathology readings while maintaining accuracy.
- Product X uses machine learning to improve outcomes for breast cancer patients.

There's no emotive connection to be found in any of those options. The audience may hang with you for a bit, but they're probably not all-in. Worst case, they may leave before you ever get to the point.

### Sticky middle

The middle of a concert—or a story—is prime exit ramp territory. Good bands will pepper minor hits into the middle of their set, or play an unexpected cover song, or mix loud and quiet songs to keep a good pace and bring the audience along.

Your job as storyteller is the same. You must maintain the

audience connection throughout the entire piece, keeping them invested in the story as it moves along. The challenge is to feed them just the right information, at just the right time, in just the right order—and to keep it all interesting. Too much information and the story drags. Too little and the audience is lost.

I often use the word "scaffolding" to describe the steady, deliberate building of a stable platform from which the audience can connect to the story. A friend of mine calls it foot holds and toe holds—like on a climbing wall. Each foot hold or toe hold is within reach and propels the climber toward the summit. It keeps them glued to the rock face. Too close together and the motion is cumbersome rather than exhilarating. Too far apart and the climber can't grasp the next hold. They never reach the goal.

Your detailed plan will help you spread that glue. Or build that scaffolding. Or design those foot holds and toe holds. However you want to think about it, be sure to ditch your "insider" lens and think through the story as if you didn't know what was going to happen. It will help you decide how to spin it out.

### Memorable close

Now back to the concert stadium. What is the very, *very* best part of a concert? For most people, it's the climactic end, when the band chooses the most phenomenal fan-favorites to close out the show. The audience is swept up in the moment and carried along as the mood reaches a fever pitch.

And then it's over. Why? Because it leaves the audience on a high note. It leaves them satisfied. There's a buzz in the air as they head to the parking lot. They will tell people about it on Monday morning. And they will buy tickets for next year's concert.

Your story should have the same effect. It should leave them wanting more. It's not enough to tie up loose ends—you need to close with a bang. It should be worth the wait. And it should leave them wanting tickets to the next show.

A great story will grease the wheels for your sales team, and that's the point. If you can capture your customer's attention, hold on to it throughout the journey, and stick the landing, your relationship is now on new footing. You've been on a journey together. You've connected. And there's a greater chance they'll take your phone call next time you're in town.

Now let's chat about something that may seem specific to video, but it's not. A good storyteller paints pictures with words. Whether your format is written or visual, imagery has a place in every story.

## Inject the images

The human brain is amazing. It's made up of multiple neural centers that absorb information from various cues and make informed responses in the form of emotion, reasoning, balance, motor skills, learning, and so much more. The cool thing is that the brain will activate whatever mental resources are triggered in order to interpret the information.

As a storyteller, that's an opportunity you can't pass up. You can intentionally build touchpoints in your story that activate neural centers and draw the audience in. You should work to ping as many of those parts of the brain as you can. In particular, zoom in on the senses—vision, hearing, smell, taste, and touch—to increase the audience connection.

Let's say there's a ball in your story. Simply referring to a ball doesn't give the brain much to grab on to, but what if you change the description to a large red shiny ball? That helps a little bit. What about the feel? The smell? We could describe how it's almost too slick to hold on to and smells like plastic. Now there are more connection points. Is the ball so full of air that it feels taut? Or is it deflated and squishy? Does it make a dull sound when it hits the wall? Or does it make a loud pop that echoes through the old, musty gymnasium? The more detailed the description, the more clearly your brain will imagine the ball and how it fits into the scene.

Imagery is not just a video thing—imagery is a storytelling thing. It's a literary tool that you can use to your advantage. The human brain doesn't require a visual image in order to conjure up a picture. Or a smell. Or taste, sound, or texture. *You have control over how deeply your audience will be immersed in the story because you push the levers that make the mental connection.* The more sensory hooks you can add, the more you can light up the listener's brain— which helps the image come into focus and the connection to deepen.

Well, that's the last of the universal tools of the trade that we're going to cover. In the next section, we'll examine some techniques that are specific to literary content. How do you choose the right words—in the right order—to make a lasting impression? How do you conform to the rules of literary excellence without becoming stodgy and stale? And how do you ensure that the impression you leave is the one you wanted to create?

**Fingertip reminders**

### Use a measuring stick

Below is the checklist that I keep front-of-mind as I'm searching for a main character, sculpting a storyline, or polishing a piece. It gives me something to measure against, and keeps the goal firmly planted within my field of view.

- Interest – Does the topic appeal to a broad audience?
- Intensity – Will they care a lot?
- Impact – Will the levels of Interest and Intensity combine to place your story in the top-right section of the Impact Quadrant?

- Compelling characters – Will they bring the story to life with their experiences, mindset, and voice?
- Engaging – Does your style draw people in?
- Captivating – Does the story develop in a way that holds the audience's attention from beginning to end?
- Surprising – Are there twists and turns along the way?
- Memorable – Have you built in elements that will cause the audience to remember the story long after the last scene has ended?
- Inspiring – Will the accumulated effect be enough to inspire action?

### Establish the tone

Establish the tone at the beginning of the process and let it influence everything from interview questions to shot design. Is your story hopeful or resigned? Tough or tender?

### Spread the glue

Work hard to create and maintain a bond between the audience and the story. You can use these pointers to help your audience stay connected:

- Emotive opener – Open with an attention-getter that draws the audience into the story.
- Sticky middle – Create connection points throughout the story that enable the audience to grab hold and move forward.
- Memorable close – Leave them wanting more.

### *Inject the images*

Add sensory hooks throughout the story—vision, hearing, smell, taste, touch—to activate the audience's neural centers. The horse might be brown—or he might be a gentle, sway-backed sorrel with large brown eyes, a rough coat, and the loudest whinny in the barn.

# LITERARY EXCELLENCE

THE FIRST RULE of language is to make it comprehensible. To connect with the audience, transmit the message, and ensure it is understood. We will start by examining your choice of words—the building blocks of language. Then we will take a look at a few time-honored tools to help you improve your technique.

## Watch your language!

Words are the raw materials you use to shape your story. You can mold them to transmit far more than information. Words reflect the mood of the story and reveal every subtle nuance of meaning. You can choose words that are bold or soft. Personal or common. Expressive or dull. The words you choose can either draw the reader toward the next page—or simply take up space.

Application matters too. Words can add dimension to the story—or cause it to deflate. Without skilled application, all of the pieces may be there, but your story won't leave the ground. It will be flat. Uninteresting. Storytellers, like any good craftsperson, must become adept at handling the tools of their trade.

Words are so important that we're going to devote the next two sections to their study. First we will explore how to choose just the right word to nail a description or pinpoint an idea. Then we will talk about how to apply those words for the strongest impact.

## Specificity rules

Choose words that express exactly what you want to say. Be intentional, specific, and descriptive. Let's start with the sentence below:

> The pudgy little boy rounded the curve from the back of the house and walked through the newly-planted flowerbed.

What can you tell about the little boy's attitude? Not much. He is placing one foot in front of the other, probably at a moderate pace. That's it. He's just walking along and he kept right on walking through the flowerbed.

Now read the modified sentence below. I have changed one word. How has your perception changed?

> The pudgy little boy rounded the curve from the back of the house and *sauntered* through the newly-planted flowerbed.

The little tyke sounds a bit aimless, huh? Like he's paying absolutely no attention. The verb is more descriptive and it helps us form a better picture. The reader is able to combine this information with additional cues from surrounding words to fill in the details. This is an important point. Words don't live independently. *Descriptive words in one part of the sentence play off words in another part of the sentence to form a more complete picture.*

The sentence doesn't tell you how old the boy is, but it does say that he's little and pudgy and he saunters. Hmm, he's probably less than three years old since he's still chubby. Still a toddler, but probably over one. One-year-olds don't saunter—careen would be more accurate. I now have a mental image of a two-year-old meandering around the corner of the house, possibly having drifted away from the watchful eye of an adult. He pays no attention to where he's stepping because that's what two-year-olds do. There's no willful destructive intent—just a pudgy little toddler aimlessly sauntering through the flowerbed.

Now let's change the verb again.

The pudgy little boy rounded the curve from the back of the house and *plowed* through the newly-planted flowerbed.

Uh-oh, now he's picking up speed. This little dude is on the run. I'm guessing he's hot-footing it away from an adult because he knows darn well he's supposed to stay in the back yard. He jolly well doesn't want to though, so he's made his escape.

Did you notice that "rounded the curve from the back of the house" took on a different slant as soon as we changed the verb from "sauntered" to "plowed"? This little guy's committed and he's not slowing down for anything. He's probably leaning into the curve a little as he takes the corner. He's determined to make his escape.

Word choice is so important. You are communicating more than facts, so slow down when you write. Be precise. Make sure the words you choose convey exactly what you have in mind.

A thesaurus can help if you use it appropriately. Every writer uses a thesaurus to jog their memory every once in a while. It can be a great tool, but choosing just the right word requires a fair amount of discernment.

Try looking up "fickle" in a thesaurus and you might find "flighty." So which is the best word to use? It depends. Synonyms are similar, but they are not exact replacements. Let's say you have a teenage character. How *exactly* might you want to characterize their attitude? Are they fickle? Or flighty?

This is where specificity helps. What is your teenager really like? Do they feel one way on Monday and another way on Tuesday? That's not unusual for a teenager—and they're certainly fickle—but does it mean they're likely to hop the next bus out of town? Probably not. They may be fickle, but they're probably not flighty. There's a big difference between the two words, despite being synonyms.

"Temperamental" is also on the list of synonyms for "fickle," but is that the right choice? If the teenager is petulant or cranky it might be. Or they might just be likely to change their mind— in which case you're back to "fickle."

A good thesaurus offers a lovely smorgasbord of words with a variety of nuances ready for the picking, but it can't do the choosing for you. The best a thesaurus can do is remind you of options that might not be front-of-mind. Words are never plug-and-play, and the overuse or misuse of a thesaurus can overwhelm an author's voice or convey a message that wasn't intended. The best use of a thesaurus opens up a wide variety of options from which to choose the exact right word.

### Those shady words

Shady. Does it mean up to no good? Or a respite from the glaring sun? Depends. The original meaning is offering shade, but the word has taken on a lot of nuance since its debut.

Imagine you are trudging the backwaters of some hot and dusty foreign country. You're tired, your feet are hot, it's approaching dinnertime, and sunset is still hours away. The guidebook says there's a hotel about two miles up the road and describes it as "shady." Hmm. Will you find welcome relief from the heat? Or will you be killed? There's a big difference.

Words come packed with meaning—and sometimes there's more in the package than you bargained for. Often they have more than one definition, including a more formal literal meaning—the denotation—and another meaning that carries either positive or negative associations—the connotation.

The connotation is the meaning that comes with a lot of baggage. The one that drags emotion or judgment along with it. These are the words that have been around the block a few times and picked up a few back stories. "Cheap" might literally mean inexpensive—or it could mean poor quality. "Cool" might mean moderately cold, or it could mean approval or admiration. If you're in slang territory there are other options as well, such as dope, GOAT, snatched, or Gucci. Don't use the slang options though. They will be gibberish for half the population and quickly outdated for the other half, which will make you out-of-touch with pretty much everyone.

On the other hand, connotative words are fair game. Sometimes they're informal enough to be considered a figure of speech, but often they find their way into the mainstream and appear in the dictionary right alongside the original. Typically the denotation holds the top spot and the connotation will be a second or third meaning.

I love using connotative options. They have layers of meaning that you can leverage to paint a vivid picture more easily—and often more succinctly—than with a literal approach.

Check out this denotative example:

*Jack has a careless and disengaged attitude at work, which makes his coworkers disinterested in forming a friendship with him.*

Now compare to this connotative option:

*Jack's lackadaisical attitude alienates his coworkers.*

Connotative words and phrases are power-packed choices because you can use them to add detail without adding words. They can make your style more engaging if you apply them intentionally and clearly.

Now we'll shift from words that are broadly understood to words that are narrow in scope.

### Industry-speak

It makes perfect sense to use industry terms when speaking to industry insiders, but as soon as you decide to create a story, the rules change. Instead of speaking to a narrow audience with industry-specific language, you are now speaking to everyone using common language. The words you choose should be easily understood by everyone from a scientist to a bartender to a programmer.

The term "technobabble" didn't find its place in Webster's without good reason. Most industries have their own lexicon, and it's simply not reasonable to expect the rest of the world to understand industry-specific terms. Nor is it polite to use them.

Your audience can't possibly follow along if you're speaking gibberish—and that's exactly what industry-speak sounds like to a general audience. For example, *de novo* would immediately be recognized as "anew" to anyone in the legal profession, yet it's more likely to have the rest of us hitting up Google. Python will conjure up images of a slithering snake in most brains, yet a data scientist will immediately recognize it as a programming language.

Industry-speak is a bit like tribal language indigenous to a small remote island—it only makes sense to other islanders. Tribal language makes for smooth communication among those who are part of the tribe, but it's not very useful for tourists. If you want your story to resonate with a broad audience, it's best to assume you're speaking to the tourists.

### Those clever acronyms

Acronyms are another common pitfall. The business world loves them. There's even an acronym to describe three-letter acronyms (TLAs). I have sat in meetings at Microsoft thinking I was the only one that didn't understand the acronym-laced vocabulary until I finally got brave enough to ask. It turned out I wasn't alone. No one else in the room—including the folks making liberal use of the acronym—knew what it stood for. They just knew it referenced a program that did so-and-so.

I have seen the same scenario in the healthcare industry. Program names are a frequent culprit. An acronym might be used to simplify a long program name, then the acronym lives on long after the words are forgotten. It's confusing enough in-house, but it's meaningless to everyone else. And sure, not all industry acronyms are detached from their meaning, yet they may still represent insider language.

If you want your audience to understand your story, speak in *their* language. Business storytellers have enough hurdles to clear without throwing up barriers of their own making. When it comes to vocabulary, it's best to shy away from both industry lingo and acronyms.

## *Fissiparousness*

Speaking of unintelligible language, obscure words aren't your best bet either. I'm not a fan of dumbed-down language—after all, words are our primary medium for storytelling and there are *so* many good ones—but choosing terms that are cryptic to most of the population is counterproductive.

When a listener encounters a word they don't understand, their mind immediately shifts away from the story and toward the word. Best case, they're distracted and no longer immersed in the story. Worst case, they're either in pursuit of a dictionary or have simply moved on to something else. Either way, you have lost your audience. (Note: fissiparous is a really cool word. I just wouldn't put it in a business story.)

Time-bound vocabulary is another culprit. Whether ancient or current day, time-bound words have relevance only within a certain timeframe. If your listener isn't from the age in which the word was popular, you're back to the gibberish problem. For example, "cattywampus" and "whopper-jawed" are colorful choices, but your audience might track your story better if you simply said "askew." "Dope" might mean a fool, or drugs, or excellent—depending on the decade. Even intuitive labels lose their connection over time. "Pine overcoat" resonates far less since cremation has come into vogue, while "left me on read" makes perfect sense—for now. After a while, it's all malarkey.

So far we've ruled out obscure, obsolete, and trendy language, but that's not all. Avoid the overused words too.

## When punchy becomes stale

Today's most popular words and phrases may actually be too faddish to carry much meaning. Even worse, using words that are too trendy can make you appear shallow—and that's a bad look for any storyteller.

One of our main goals in marketing is to differentiate our brand from the competition, and we can't do that by sounding like everyone else. There's nothing unique about using an overworn word.

My nomination for the number one term to strike off your list? Transformation. It's clearly past its prime. Everyone, it seems, has transformed something in the last decade.

Top of the online search list:

- Weight loss
- Dry cleaning
- Airport security
- Car wash
- Your life (because . . . why not?)
- Digital transformation (537 million hits alone)
- And my personal favorite—Beachbody On Demand's Transform 2.0

There was a time when transformation was punchy, but that was a good while ago. Early-2010s was its heyday. It may come back into fashion—these things tend to be cyclical—but for now, it's time to give it a rest. And there are plenty of other candidates that could use a rest, such as enable, empower, and paradigm. They've all been around the block a few too many times.

The words may vary, but the rule is consistent: as soon as

everybody else is using a word, it's time to find a new one. All is not lost, though. You can find another approach if you dig a little deeper. Look for specificity. Instead of using "transform," tell your audience *how* you are transforming. Are you transcending a broken system? Annihilating roadblocks? Reviving the industry?

When it comes to word choice, don't lean on a popular word past its prime no matter how great it is. There are better ways to differentiate your brand than to sound like everyone else. Start by being one of the first to relegate overused words to the dustbin of marketing history and refocus on what your brand does best. Heck, you might even be the first to popularize the next great marketing word. That's a far better position than bobbing along in a crowded sea of followers.

## Device advice

Now let's cover some tried-and-true techniques to boost your writing. You may have run into some of these as early as First Grade, but they're worth a review to help bring them into practice.

### *Alliteration*

Let's start by backing up to the previous sentence. Instead of "tried-and-true techniques" I could have said "popular techniques" or "literary devices." Both of those phrases are accurate—but they aren't as recognizable and they don't land the same punch.

Why not? The repetitive "t" sound at the beginning of multiple words draws attention to itself. It adds an element of rhythm and gives the brain something to hold on to. And it brings a bit of attitude too. It's percussive.

Alliteration is a simple yet powerful tool that you can use in your writing. Some folks define alliteration as the repetitive use of the same sound at the beginning of multiple words. Like this: *"The ball bounced behind the bleachers."*

Others insist it's the accent that counts rather than the beginning of the word. The idea is to place the repetitive sound on emphasized syllables—whether they're at the beginning of the word or not. Like this: *"Friends and foes can both deflate a fancy ego."* Here the "f" in "deflate" occurs on the accented syllable and contributes to the punch.

Personally I'm a fan of strong, percussive consonants on accented syllables, but you can choose what appeals most to your ear. You can use vowels too. Like this: *"Alluring melodies allude to the lurid life of loose morals."* Pardon the judgment, but the effect is obvious. It's all about establishing an aural rhythm to your writing, which is why two different letter combinations— "u" and "oo"—work just fine. It's not about the look; it's about the sound.

Now let's apply the technique to marketing. Check out this snippet of fictitious marketing copy:

*Product X reduces expenditures while maintaining quality.*

And here's the same message with alliteration:

*Product X controls costs without compromising quality.*

Alliteration has a ring to it. A rhythm that brings emphasis to certain words. It enters your mind easier, translates into meaning faster, and sticks there longer. Used judiciously, it can be a powerful tool—assuming it makes its way through review cycles intact. Don't be surprised if your alliteration gets red-lined. Sometimes reviewers unintentionally obliterate carefully designed copy in favor of preferred words or phrases.

This is one of those places where you don't want to give up your role as writer. Uncontrolled review cycles without a literary voice can turn the copy into a potpourri of popular words. Part of your job as storyteller is to hang tough, take the blows, stand back up, and get back in the game. If you don't, the final copy is likely to have a writing-by-committee flavor—which is never good.

Make the feedback process a conversation. Find out why the copy changed—was it for accuracy, clarity, or word choice—then explain that you're trying to maintain the alliteration. If the problem was accuracy or clarity, this is probably the reviewer's domain and you're going to need to flex. If it was word choice, you may be best qualified to make the final decision.

If you're a writer, don't abdicate your responsibility to write. Always offer your insight. Consider the review process a collaboration where everyone brings their expertise to the table rather than a grin-and-bear-it exercise in imploding prose.

### Parallel structure

Imagine you're part of a project that has had trouble gaining traction. The objectives are clear, but the progress has been minimal. There's a meeting this afternoon. You check the calendar notes and this is what you see:

> This afternoon we will talk about how to make the most progress from here on out. We have faced many hurdles and we need to talk about what those are and how to get around them. Ideally, we will align on how to move forward.

Sounds a bit wishy-washy, doesn't it? It certainly doesn't instill a ton of confidence. And it's way too long. It's tough to extract concrete meeting goals from those words—which feels like the project will continue to flail. But what if it sounded more like this?

We will spend time this afternoon identifying hurdles, exploring alternatives, and committing to solutions that will get us back on track.

Bam. Now I get it. Three steps to success. What's the difference? The second example says substantially the same thing, but it uses parallel structure. Simply speaking, parallel structure is the repetition of a grammatical form within a sentence or list.

Let's take a peek. Here are the three phrases that all have the same structure:

- Identifying hurdles
- Exploring alternatives
- Committing to solutions

Each option could live on its own in the same functional pattern. We could say, "We will spend time this afternoon *identifying hurdles*" or we could say, "We will spend time this afternoon *exploring alternatives.*" Not to belabor the point, but we could also say, "We will spend time this afternoon *committing to solutions.*" Each phrase has the same grammatical structure and performs the same function.

Once again, rhythm and repetition add clarity and clout. They make it easier for the brain to extract meaning and retain it. Parallel structure helps your writing be more understandable, often in fewer words. And it adds punch.

Personally, I find that parallel elements in a sentence work best in threes. That's not a hard and fast rule, but it's a good first approach.

## Similes and metaphors

Now let's take a look at similes and metaphors. Famous authors from William Shakespeare to Maya Angelou have used the technique with great success. Musicians use them too.

The song "Life is a Highway"[14] isn't about a literal road—it's about a metaphorical journey, and how our lives are built for travel. We move from (literal or figurative) place to place, connecting with people and experiences along the way. The next day—or week, or year—we move on to new people and new experiences. Sometimes we revisit old destinations. Sometimes our road takes us another direction.

And here's one of my favorite literary metaphors:

> *"Well, you keep away from her,*
> *cause she's a rattrap if I ever seen one."*
>
> John Steinbeck, *Of Mice and Men*

Whoa. Rattrap, huh? Seems a bit harsh. It communicates a lot though. A rattrap is large—bigger than a mousetrap—and it wields a lot of power. A rattrap entices the unwary with alluring bait, then snaps shut with a clap. It's final too. There's no escape once the trap has sprung.

All of that meaning in one word—the woman is alluring, enticing, powerful, quick, deadly, and final. Meanwhile, the man is unwary. Clueless perhaps. Sounds like a bad situation for sure.

Similes and metaphors are similar devices, but not exactly the same. They're easy to distinguish though. A metaphor says one thing *is* another, while a simile says one thing is *like*—or similar to—another. They achieve the same objective, but a simile is a little softer than a metaphor.

Both vehicles are used to make a statement. Steinbeck says

the woman is a rattrap, Skittles tells us to taste the rainbow, and Red Bull gives us wings—or at least they used to. State Farm uses a simile to make a softer comparison by saying it is *like* a good neighbor. None of these statements are literal, but they're all effective.

When you're trying to get a point across, consider comparing it to something the audience knows and understands well. A simile or metaphor will provide an instant connection.

Well, that's it for techniques that are specific to literary content. It's not comprehensive by any means, but mastering these tools will make your writing a bit sharper.

Next we'll talk about video content, but first a few reminders.

 **Fingertip reminders**

Words are the raw materials you use to convey your message, so be deliberate about which ones you choose and how you string them together.

### Do this:

- Specificity – Choose words that are intentional, specific, and descriptive. Did the little boy *walk*, *saunter*, or *plow* through the flowerbed?

- Connotations – Pack more meaning into words and phrases by leveraging the implied meaning. Do you want to portray your product as cheap or affordable?

- Alliteration – Use rhythm and repetition to give your copy more clarity and clout.

- Parallel structure – Use a repetitive grammatical formula to make your writing more understandable.

For example: We will spend this afternoon *identifying hurdles, exploring alternatives, and committing to solutions.*

- Similes and Metaphors – Deploy comparative language to make a power-packed point. Think of Steinbeck referring to a woman as a "rattrap" or the song, "Life is a Highway."

### Don't do this:

- Industry-speak – Drop all industry terms. Your storytelling audience is everyone, so everyone should understand the language.

- Acronyms – Spell out acronyms, except those that are widely recognizable, such as CEO or USA.

- Obscure vocabulary – Avoid words that may be cryptic to much of the population. This is not the time to stretch anyone's vocabulary.

- Overused words – Retire overly popular words. Once everyone else is using a word, it's time to find a new one.

# VIDEO KNOW-HOW

I F YOU'RE INTO business storytelling, chances are you're into video. People watch videos for entertainment, for information, and yes—for marketing. They're twice as likely to share the content too.[15]

Video content gives you a bigger reach. Audiences *love* video and they're watching more every day. Currently people are spending 3.25 *billion* hours watching YouTube videos every month—up 60% from last year.[16] That's nuts. And a good reason for you to perfect your video storytelling skills.

## Choose the best voice

Once you decide on your characters and your storyline, it's time to think about delivery. With video, you have a decision to make on who's going to deliver the script. Are you going to use interview style? Voiceover? How about dialogue? Let's take a look at some of the options.

### Interview

When you find a main character with a deeply personal story, let them be the one to tell it on camera. No other method can match the authenticity. No one else will feel the weight of the outcome or deliver the raw emotion like the person who lived it. Don't worry if they're not polished or formal—that's not their job. The main character's job is to reveal the heartache and joy of their journey. That's it.

If you decide to interview the main character, stick with that style throughout the video. That means the hero (customer) and mentor (your company) will also appear as "talking heads." The corporate characters will most likely present themselves as polished, but don't force an artificial delivery. You should work to portray the customer and internal voices as professional, but not detached. Ensure the customer validates the role of the solution, but don't insist that they parrot key messages word-for-word. It won't land well.

Interview style gives you the greatest potential to humanize your story, but it doesn't come without risk. The biggest downside is that you need to make sure each character delivers every element of the storyline—in words that pass legal review—without a script. I find it to be the most stressful part of the shoot, but it can be done well if you're working hand-in-hand with a great director. And if you have done your homework.

The worst case scenario is returning from a video shoot with a bunch of footage and trying to fashion a storyline out of the interview. Don't do that. Make sure you have a detailed plan, and then follow it. The video interview shouldn't uncover any surprises. If it does, you haven't prepared well enough.

Remember where the video shoot falls in the process. Most of the work has already been done.

- Conduct exploratory research
- Identify a human conflict, cast of characters, and key points
- Conduct targeted research
- Design detailed plan

- Write article or *shoot video*
- Review and polish
- Publish

By the time you get to the shoot you're already intimately familiar with the story. You have a rapport with each of the characters. You have done your product research and your customer research. You have spoken to each character, usually multiple times, so you know that their speech is intelligible. You have dug deep and designed the best possible storyline. You have created a detailed plan that calls out each element you are going to capture in an interview and who will speak to it. You have crafted interview questions. You know the tone of the story and what visuals you will capture to support the script.

Once you get on-site, your challenge is to capture a smooth, authentic delivery with just the right inflections. This responsibility falls squarely on the director, so make sure you have chosen well, and remember your role during the interview. A good director will work to establish a connection and a level of raw transparency that is irreplaceable. Be sure not to snap that connection. If you're missing a key point in your wireframe and they're just not getting around to it, write yourself a note and wait for the director to break before you bring it up.

I like to have a working rhythm with the director that leaves their focus largely uninterrupted, yet also has planned touch points so we can chat about what might be mangled or missing. That is your on-set job as storyteller—you're the consultant that makes sure every box is ticked so when you get to the editing phase you have everything you need to tell an amazing story. If you identify a hiccup or a point that is missing, the director can rephrase the question or remind the character of your previous phone conversation.

## *Voiceover*

Interview-style videos are great, but they're not the only choice. A voiceover script can be a great option, especially if you've created a hypothetical scenario, you're dealing with a heavy accent or language barrier, or you don't have direct control over the shoot.

Lack of hands-on production control has massive implications for your approach. One of those is script delivery. Here's an example:

One of the videos I managed for Microsoft was targeted for their Worldwide Partner Conference. It was a complicated international shoot and even though I make it a point to attend every video shoot, this one was going to be tough. We needed to film in a region of Nigeria where Boko Haram was an active terrorist threat. It was particularly dangerous for Westerners, women, and journalists—or anyone hauling around a camera—and I was a dead-ringer for all three. I was out.

The agency video crew was out too. It seems no one's family—not to mention the insurance company—was keen to have the crew make the trip. With none of us on the ground, that meant we had to hire and manage a remote video crew to capture the footage.

There were three locations in Nigeria—a health clinic, a school, and a local power company—and with all of the moving parts and lack of hands-on production control, there was no way we could effectively manage a video interview. So we ditched the interview and made plans for a professional voiceover. Meanwhile, we provided detailed instruction to a videographer from an adjacent African country to capture the footage.

The shoot days came and went. We heard word that the

videographer had shown up for the shoot, but then he dropped off the grid. Total silence. The video agency couldn't reach him and neither could any of our contacts in Nigeria. Two weeks and tons of unanswered emails and phone calls later, the footage showed up one day on a cloud site we had set up weeks prior.

If ever there was a video that screamed for a professional voiceover, this was it. Our ability to manage the on-site experience was extremely limited. The variety of speaking accents alone would have made it difficult to manage even if we'd been able to secure the interviews, but a voiceover worked great. We hired excellent professional talent and the video was ready in time for the event.

Your reasons for creating a voiceover don't have to be so dramatic. Voiceovers are a great approach for high-altitude visionary pieces, fictional storylines, and stories with non-English speaking characters or those with heavy accents. And sometimes you might simply make a creative call, such as when the storyline demands a voice that can lend gravitas to the delivery.

### Dialogue

Dialogue is another option that can work well—if it's executed properly. Every approach has its challenges, but dialogue in particular can sound artificial or come across as amateurish if it's not done right. Believable dialogue is heavily dependent on two things: the script and the talent.

On the script, make sure you're working with a writer who can write dialogue. Casual speech is very different from formal speech, such as a presentation or a voiceover. The lines needs to sound "real," which is easier said than done.

The dialogue also needs to fit naturally into realistic surroundings. If your scene calls for a child to walk into the room, the script needs to acknowledge their presence. What parent ignores their child to prattle on about some new product? If the boss walks by, it might force a change in topic or tone. Maybe they wind up quickly and turn their attention to an upcoming meeting. These subtle acknowledgments of humanity make your scene feel real.

Talent auditions are a must, and in-person is best. I suggest you use a respectable talent agency and study the actors' bios. Talent with both stage and film experience is a plus, but be leery of stage-only. Stage acting requires a more exaggerated delivery than film, so you could run into issues with overacting. A good film actor can convey a ton of meaning with a raised eyebrow that wouldn't even be noticed on-stage.

Kids are another danger zone. They can be high reward, but they're also high risk. I've seen an adorable three-year-old add an amazing "aaaaawwww" factor to a video—and I've seen an awkward delivery from a child completely destroy an otherwise great video.

An additional word of warning: if someone suggests their best friend's kid or their next-door neighbor, don't consider it unless they're an accredited actor. Stick with talent that has agency representation. If any one of your hired talent misses the mark, the whole video will tank.

## Focus the lens

Now that you have a voice for your video, let's talk about the visuals. Don't waste them. Don't limit yourself to visuals that mimic exactly what is said in the script or you will leave much of their power untouched.

### *See and say*

If your main character fell during a health episode, you don't need to actually show them falling. Maybe they were getting ready for work when they fell—you can show a close-up of fingers buttoning a shirt. Their thoughtful expression. Then shift to talking head and capture the complexity of feelings on their face as they speak about going to the hospital. This is an emotional reminiscence—you don't need an ambulance with red lights. And you definitely don't need stock ambulance footage that doesn't match the native shots.

A great director of photography (DP) and director will team up to creatively capture visuals that do more than a replay—they actually tell part of the story. Rely on their expertise. Done right, the script and visuals will play off of each other. Light coming through the trees might tell us the plot is about to take a turn—even though there are no trees in the script.

Learn to tell the story with pictures and your story will be stronger. Test yourself. Watch your video on mute. How much story do you get from the visuals? Not just what they're *doing*, but what they're *feeling*. Can you tell when the main character is struggling? Can you pinpoint the turn when your character senses victory? Do the visuals elicit emotion? Do they move the audience from peace to turmoil to joy? Are they beautiful to watch? Is your eye drawn to the screen?

Now do the same with the script. Listen with your eyes closed. Are there holes in the story that make it hard to follow? Do the vocal inflections reveal the mood?

Now watch the full video. Do the script and visuals work together to tell the story? They should. *The script and visuals should partner together to tell a story that is stronger than the sum of its parts.*

## A matter of ~~urgency~~ agency

This may all sound overwhelming, but remember that you're not in it alone. Once you have found your main character and know their story, it's your job to choose the very best video team and work hand-in-hand with them to bring the story to life. To do that, you need to understand the basics of video production, speak their language, and be the bridge between the video crew and the product. You should plan to be heavily involved with the video team to create a rock-solid wireframe, be the on-set consultant, and give detailed feedback during edit cycles.

### *Who are these people anyway?*

There are standard roles in video production. Let's start with the producer. This is the person that makes sure the project goes smoothly. Need a cool location to shoot a scene? They'll source some options and arrange a scout. Need furniture with the right vibe to put in that location? They'll figure that out too—all while coordinating with the director and DP for the right look. And talent auditions. And travel. And your interface with the crew. And whatever else needs done. This is the puppet master who makes sure everything from the airline tickets to the potted plant arrive on time, in place, and within budget. The producer will be your main contact for a video project.

Next is the director. This is the person who will extract just the right words in just the right tone with just the right setting to tell your story. Partner with them ahead of time on a detailed plan. Discuss tone, personalities, high points, and low points. Then ping the plan back and forth until both of you are happy. Once you're on-set, give the director whatever support they need to bring that plan to life. If you need to stay out of the way, stay out of the way. If you need to communicate a concern, do it now. You can't fix everything in editing.

Your DP is essentially an artist with a camera. There may be additional camerapersons on-site, but the DP is running the show. Be sure to give them the creative license to use their talent. Chances are they will vary wide, medium, and close camera shots. They will change the angle and height. The shot might be static or it could be moving. They might use a tripod, dolly, or handheld. They might move with the handheld or they might stay in one place. The subject might walk onto the screen or already be there when the shot opens. They might shoot match cuts. Top shots. A cut-in, cutaway, or swipe.

The list is long and you don't have to master their bag of tricks, but you should know enough to be part of the conversation. The more you learn their language, the better storytelling partner you will be—just don't interrupt their work to ask.

Do you know what a match cut is? You have probably seen one in a movie. Let's say a person is standing in the kitchen and lifts a glass of orange juice to their lips, then the scene shifts to them standing in a gym lowering a water bottle away from their lips. The up motion of the glass takes place in the kitchen in office clothes—the down motion of the water bottle takes place in the gym in workout clothes. It's a seamless way to move time and location. The point is—you don't have to know all the ins and outs of videography, but you should hire someone who does and be curious enough to learn and be part of the conversation.

Once the project is in the can, it's the editor's turn. They will work their magic on all those hours of raw footage. The match cut will come together. They might punch in to emphasize a certain element in a scene—or select a wide shot to introduce the next scene. They might patch together scenes with swipe shots, select a top shot, or replace a screenshot on a monitor with a completely different image—all while the distance and angle are shifting.

An editor can do crazy stuff with audio too. They can space words further apart or closer together. They can create a new sentence from several different phrases. And they can lay down a music track and align the different elements to match the action on the screen.

### *Top-notch teams*

So how do you select the video team that will bring your story to life? All production teams are not alike. Some are internal with a slew of experience cranking out informational videos. Some are creative agencies with an afterthought video wing. Some are hobbyists turned pro. Some come from a journalistic background while others lean toward the movie industry. Some love the storytelling process, while others like the video gear.

Finding the right agency is critical. So how do you do it? How do you find an agency that has the right talent and training to help you deliver knock-out videos?

1.  Find a *video* agency. Not just an agency that will hire a freelance crew. Track down an agency that specializes in video and has as many in-house resources as possible.

2.  If they tell you they specialize in case studies, run like the wind. Case studies and stories are two different animals, and if the agency doesn't understand the difference—or thinks that layering storytelling techniques on top of case studies changes them into stories—that's a bad sign.

3. Look for specialized education. If the core crew members have bothered to go to school for their craft, chances are they have the passion, commitment, and expertise you're looking for. Bonus points if they have experience in independent film. It's a great telltale sign that they're serious, and they're good.

4. Think twice before hiring a run-and-gun agency birthed from talk shows or news programs. Those crews are literally designed for flash-in-the-pan attention, and it may be difficult for them to pivot toward well-developed, cohesive, high-impact stories.

5. Ask to see a *variety* of video styles from their portfolio. You're looking for creativity. Innovation. If you find cookie-cutter content, that's a no-go. Also, watch out for amateur moves like a subject positioned in front of a window so that the view is washed-out, the subject's face is too dark, and there's a plant coming out of their head.

6. Finally, meet with them. Face-to-face if possible. Explain an upcoming project and see where they go. If it's excitement, a multiplicity of ideas, and eagerness to show you really interesting examples, you've found your agency. If not, keep looking. You'll be really glad you did.

### Resource allocation

Now that you have an amazing video team, make sure to give them the resources they need to do an amazing job. Budget for video is tricky. The cost for a three minute video can vary widely because the ingredients vary widely. And—like most things you buy—the ingredients make all the difference.

Let's talk pizza for a minute. Imagine you're on a quest to find the very best pizza in town. Do you think your chances are better at the Mexican-Italian-Greek buffet that uses frozen dough, tear-open toppings, clumpy cheese, and a low-temperature oven? Or at the family-owned Italian restaurant that makes their dough in-house, uses fresh ingredients, imports the very best cheese, and bakes in a wood-fired oven? Would you assume that the only difference in a large Margherita pizza from the two different locations is price?

The point is—video agencies don't all have the same level of expertise, nor do they use the same ingredients. Even if you're working with a top-notch team, they probably have a range of equipment and personnel they can assign to your job.

If you see two quotes from two different agencies and each of them says they will conduct a two-day shoot, allow three review cycles, and deliver a three-minute video—that doesn't mean the two are comparable. And if you give the higher-priced agency a chance to meet the lower quote, chances are they can sub cheaper personnel and gear and match it. If the quote is too low, you may find that a reputable agency will turn it down because they don't want to crank out a suboptimal product.

If you want the best result, use an expert team, allow adequate time for planning and scouting, include however many production days they need to do a bang-up job, and let them use their best gear. This doesn't mean that the budgetary sky is the limit, but don't expect a great video if you insist on cheap ingredients.

Give the green light for a budget that supports multiple cameras and make sure they're the best cameras you can afford. Let them use automated camera dollies so the eye doesn't see a static picture. Pay for a set designer if you need it. The same for location fees. Spring for an extra monitor or two so you can see what's going on without being the annoying person who's leaning over their shoulder while they're trying to work. And most importantly, don't squeeze so hard that you get the assistant producer, the novice director, the DP intern, and the hobbyist editor on your team.

### The shots

Now that you have a great team, use their expertise to capture the visuals. First, rely on your DP and director to find a beautiful setting for the shoot. There's no reason for your audience to see anything but beauty across the entire length of the video. If you have a crack video team—and you should—they will want to scout ahead of time. If they're able to scout at least one day prior, they may haul in a few props to dress the set. If they shoot same-day, they may drag some things from other locations to improve the shot. Let them do their job. If your video team is happy with the setup, chances are you'll be happy with the visuals.

Word of advice: if your video team is okay with shooting a customer sitting at their cluttered desk backed up to a dirty window with the harsh overhead lights overwhelming their face—find a different video team. Sounds ridiculous, but I'm not kidding. I've seen plenty of those ugly shots in customer videos. The same for a sterile hallway or an ugly conference room shot.

Second, capture great footage of each talking head, but don't plan on showing it endlessly in the final video. There's nothing terribly interesting about watching a person talk. What is far more interesting are visuals that add depth to the words that are coming out of the speaker's mouth, so make sure the team shoots gorgeous b-roll that reflects the mood across every bit of the story. That way you can show glimpses of the speaker to maintain cohesion without relying too heavily on talking head visuals.

## Edit cycles

Now let's assume that you've made it through the video shoot in fine form. The speaker didn't stammer, there's tons of beautiful footage, and it's time to put it all together.

Despite your best intentions, it can all go south during editing. Imagine the job from the editor's point of view. This is job #13473, they just downloaded nine hours of footage, and the first draft of a three-minute video is due in eight days.

There's no way they're going to get this right without a ton of context. The producer, director, and perhaps the DP all play a role. The producer will manage the workflow, communications, file delivery, and timeline. The DP may be involved in color correction. But it's the director who must imprint the vision for the video into the editor's brain.

The director knows every nuance of the storyline and how it played out during the interview. They know the best lines, the best scenes, and the best shots. This is the person you have spent hours collaborating with about the storyline, the tone, and the key points. You've travelled with them, talked endlessly about the role of each character, and watched over every shot. You need them to shepherd the story through editing.

Still, when you get the first cut it will most likely miss the mark here and there. I've never approved a first cut and I've never heard of anyone else approving one either. Now it's your turn to help polish the video.

Notice I said it's *your* turn. This is not the time to share the video with the broader internal team because first impressions are hard to change. The first cut—and probably the second and maybe the third—will have hiccups. You don't want to risk coloring their impression with a disappointing video when it's actually a great video that's simply not ready to share.

When you send your feedback, get picky and be specific. Comments like, "I don't like the music," don't give enough information to be helpful. On the other hand, absolute commands negate the expertise of everyone else on the team.

I typically open with general comments and then move on to specifics, being as generous with the accolades as I am with the critique. First, there's as much to learn from what you *liked* as what you *disliked*. Second, it's polite. Multiple people have spent hours and hours cutting your video down from nine hours of footage to the very best lines with the very best shots arranged in the best possible way to tell your story in three minutes. With music. Your feedback should acknowledge their work and point out the parts that hit the target well so they don't scrub them out during the next revision.

Then point out what you would like them to address. Try to give robust feedback that covers these elements:

- Where in the video you have feedback
- What you do like
- What you don't like
- Why you don't like it
- How you think it might be resolved

Everyone has their own feedback process and you will need to develop your own rhythm with the agency team. If the video is interview style, I like to nail the script first. Sometimes that's an audio cut and sometimes the editor has laid down visuals, but the primary focus of the first review is all about getting the script right. That's not always standard protocol and you don't have to do it that way, but I have found it speeds up the process in the long run and improves the end result. I will often close my eyes or stare out the window in order to concentrate completely on the words. Does it tell the story I want to tell?

Next up is a first full cut that lays visuals onto the approved script. Here's an example of how I might respond (although an actual response would likely be more extensive).

Wow, this is going to be great! Sarah is wonderful on camera. You can see the emotion on her face and hear it in her voice. The script came together beautifully and I love how you were able to map the visuals to capture the shifting mood.

A few comments below:

- 0:17 – I get the mood set, but this feels a little long before we introduce the character. Can we shorten it a bit?

- 0:56 – The storyline feels a bit jumbled here. Let's review the script and see if we can smooth it out. Can you send me an updated copy of the script? Also the full transcript where we highlighted the best lines?

- 1:02-1:32 – This is particularly good. The pensive outdoor shots are beautiful and they align great with the script. Please lock this section.

- 1:56 – A little too much talking head here. How did the garden shots come out? Anything we can use from there? Or another option?

- 2:47-2:52 – Please swap the last two shots. Let's close with the wide shot of Sarah walking away.

- 2:49 – The music swell is premature and covers the script. Please adjust.

Thank you so much for a great first cut. Please let me
know when you anticipate v-next will be available.

Collaboration is key. I don't want to be so prescriptive that I
negate the creative expertise of the team, nor do I want to be too
lazy to dig into the details. This approach allows the entire team
to operate at its very best in order to deliver the best possible
video. Plus, it's a ton of fun.

Next, we will talk about video length. How do you hit that
sweet spot that gives you time to tell a great story without being
so long that nobody wants to watch it?

## Too-long-didn't-watch

Imagine you're cruising through Netflix looking for something
to watch. You find two movies that look good. Then you notice
the length—one is three and a half hours long, while the other
is a breezy 90 minutes. Odds are your choice just got a lot
easier.

The issue of time commitment is compounded when you're
talking about a marketing video: shorter is generally better—
but only to a point. A two-minute video beats a ten-minute
video pretty much every time, but there's more to know on
both ends of the spectrum.

Let's talk long-form for a moment. Long-form was the latest
and greatest video fad a few years ago and it's still making the
rounds in some circles. I'm talking about those 8-12 minute
marketing pieces that came in with a bang and went out with a
whimper. I suppose it was an attempt at movie-making for the
business world, but it didn't seem to stick for long.

Here's how it often played out: I had a new client when long-
form was at its height, and one of my first tasks was to chop
down a brand new (and expensive) behemoth of a video into

a more manageable size—one that could actually be shown at an event or in a customer visit. Basically, something that didn't require popcorn.

Once I dug into the piece it was pretty easy to see how they had managed to make it so long. They spent four whole minutes on the setup. My client's contribution didn't even enter the picture until 4:08. The rest of the script was wandering and loose, with the same point made multiple times in a variety of ways.

I slashed the set-up, then spent most of my time tightening up the script. In the end, the video went from 8:41 to 2:12—and told the exact same story. I even showed the video to a few people who were familiar with the original piece and asked each of them to tell me what they thought was missing. Their answer? Nothing. None of them missed any of the content that had been cut. Even better, the 2:12 version found its way into a keynote at a major event.

### The sweet spot

So how long should your video be? The answer is—it depends. Statistics show that videos under 60 seconds have the highest probability of holding viewers all the way to the end, but there's more to it than that. You can't exactly tell a full-fledged story in 30 seconds.

But here's where things get interesting. It turns out—and this is an important point—that more viewers will stick with a 2-4 minute video than a 1-2 minute video.[17] That may seem counterintuitive on the surface, but not if you dig a little deeper.

The 1-2 minute variety falls in no-man's land. It's too long for a teaser and too short for a story. Any longer than 4 minutes and you risk losing your audience, but any shorter than

2 minutes and you can't do your story justice. There simply isn't adequate time to set the stage, introduce the characters, track them through twists and turns, and come to a successful, life-changing solution. Videos are a great medium for storytelling, but you need to hit the sweet spot on length.

So there's your answer. *As a rule of thumb, 2-4 minutes is a great length for storytelling videos.* Now let's talk about how to pack the best story into those 2-4 minutes.

## The high bar

The business world has a lot of video content, but it doesn't have a lot of *great* video content. There's no reason you can't change that unfortunate circumstance by applying the tools you've learned—and by avoiding some common pitfalls in content marketing.

### *Templates*

I have two words to say about templates for storytelling videos: *please don't.* No one wants to revisit the same storyline told over and over again with plug-and-play characters. Despite the consumer appetite for James Bond, Harry Potter, and Star Wars, the approach doesn't work with marketing content.

For starters, those series represent an unfolding storyline across time using the same characters as they experience new situations. That's probably not true for your projects. Your characters will change and so will their stories. Second, those movies have a huge footprint advantage. By the time they hit global release, much of the world is already familiar with them. It's highly doubtful that your videos will have that level of familiarity. And finally, in the end you are selling something and everybody knows it. Don't make the story as predictable as the outcome.

Keep your content fresh. Use the element of surprise when appropriate. Vary how you introduce the characters and how you close it out. Make some stories more dramatic and some more uplifting. Initiate each storytelling project with a strong ideation phase to choose the very best approach.

### Text

And finally, it's usually best to avoid any kind of text on the screen with the exception of the attributions and outro. If you're aiming for a cinematic delivery—and you should be— you shouldn't need kinetic text, infographics, or numbers to tell the story. This isn't a case study; it's an ultrashort movie. You don't go to a movie expecting holes in the plot to be supplied as read-along. Sure, there might be a "two years later" indicator, but not a missing point spelled out on-screen. And your story won't be number-centric, so you don't need to flash stats and metrics either.

Text in a storytelling video is typically a loud and visible announcement that you messed up. You either didn't capture essential information during the shoot, or it wasn't distilled properly in editing, or you lost an internal battle because you didn't sell everyone on the value of storytelling, so now you have to slap numbers up on the screen. Rather than adding to the story, your audience will now be distracted as they try to watch both the fancy text and the scene playing out in front of them. Don't make them choose.

**Fingertip reminders**

Video content is high value, but it's more complicated to produce than written content and requires a broader team with specialized skills.

Here's some information on voice:

- Interview style – When you find a main character with a deeply personal story, let them tell it on camera.

- Voiceover – A voiceover script can be a great option, especially if you've created a hypothetical scenario, you're dealing with a heavy accent or language barrier, or you don't have direct control over the shoot.

- Dialogue – Work with a writer who can write dialogue, and conduct auditions with professional talent.

Here are a few pointers to help you find a great production team:

- Find an agency that specializes in video and has in-house resources.

- Look for specialized education and experience in independent film.

- If they don't seem to understand the difference between a case study and a story, move on.

- Ask to see a variety of video styles from their portfolio and avoid any agency that shows you cookie-cutter content.

- And finally, meet with them. Look for excitement, a passion for story, a multiplicity of ideas, and eagerness to show you interesting examples.

And a few more pointers to get the most out of the agency you just hired:

- Allow adequate budget for the best talent and the best gear you can reasonably afford. Give the team flexibility to manage add-ons such as production days, location fees, and art direction.
- When you give feedback during the editing cycles, be as generous with the accolades as you are with the critique. Give specific notes:
  - ➤ *Where* in the video you have feedback
  - ➤ *What* you do like
  - ➤ *What* you don't like
  - ➤ *Why* you don't like it
  - ➤ *How* you think it might be resolved

And a few final tips and tricks:

- Work with your video team to capture visuals that add to the story.
- Remember that your DP is an artist with a camera. You don't have to master their bag of tricks, but you should be curious enough to learn and be part of the conversation.
- As a rough rule of thumb, 2-4 minutes is a great length for storytelling videos.

- Templates constrain creativity and limit storytelling options. Instead, initiate each project with a strong ideation phase to choose the very best approach.

- Avoid on-screen text, infographics, or numbers. Make sure that everything you need to tell the story is covered during the shoot.

# ODDS AND ENDS

AND NOW WE'LL wind up with a few remaining notes on storytelling. Let's start with a side trip to talk about all those great marketing messages we've heaved into the dustbin. What do we do about those? They're obviously important—so important that messaging frameworks have become a staple of the marketing industry. A messaging framework is where we house all of that ready-made, pre-approved copy for those [insert-here] opportunities.

I am an unadulterated fan of messaging frameworks—as long as they're used properly. But are they universally applicable at all times and in all places? No! Like any tool, they require knowledgeable application.

## Messaging . . . what is it good for?

A messaging framework provides the guidance needed to consistently put your brand's best foot forward. The process can be exhausting, but the outcome is so worth it. A framework moves your brand narrative from fuzzy to precise. Key messaging pillars are built, associated benefits are aligned to the pillars, and differentiators are called out. Proof points and competitive messages are established. Customer personas are identified and pain points addressed. Tag lines, short messages, and long messages are defined.

A good messaging framework pulls together all of your product's strongest talking points, distills them into a cohesive narrative, and gets everybody on the same page. Now, everyone from content creators to sales teams to public relations is singing the same tune.

But here's the thing. Messaging frameworks are written from a corporate point of view. They're all about the product. The language skews formal. They use a lot of numbers, and the vocabulary is often industry-specific.

Do you see the problem? It's too product-centric for a story. Too salesy. And *way* too "all about me." The messaging should come alive through the story, but not in a literal sense. While the words from a messaging framework might be perfect cut-and-paste candidates for an informative asset, they can be the death knell for an inspirational piece.

*Inspiration centers on people, while messaging revolves around product.* Inspiration requires authenticity, but messages can sound contrived—especially coming from the mouth of a customer. Sometimes they can sound downright awkward.

## The clumsy attempt

I have overseen a slew of customer video shoots with a directive to capture a specific sentence or phrase from the mouth of a customer. Often a good-hearted customer will try to play along. And while it may seem like a great idea, they rarely land the delivery. It can be nearly impossible to coax unnatural words out of a non-actor and make them sound natural.

Sometimes a seasoned executive might deliver the line well, yet it still sounds contrived. For someone less skilled, the attempt might be halting and awkward, even with a teleprompter. They stumble over words, get frustrated, and lose concentration—even if they have seen and approved the copy ahead of time.

And even when the customer does a bang-up job of delivery, the message can feel fake—mostly because it is. How on earth could your customer be well-versed enough in your messaging—and it's obviously messaging—for it to roll naturally off their tongue? Words painstakingly polished by a marketing department rarely mimic how a customer would speak.

A better way to land the message is to give the customer the latitude to make it relatable to their own experience and phrase it in their own words. The *essence* of the message can be far more powerful than asking your customer to parrot your exact phraseology. You don't want the customer to tell *your* story—you want them to tell *their* story empowered by your product or service.

Check out this fictitious message designed to be delivered by a retail clerk at a new storefront:

> "The new Point-of-Sale device boasts advanced inventory management capabilities, smarter sales and reporting, and cloud-based data management. The POS device is compatible with tap and digital wallet payments, and the cloud-hosted data is accessible from anywhere."

Now here's what might be going through the clerk's head:

> "My job has nothing to do with cloud-based data management or reporting. I get paid to make customers happy and sell lots of product. That's it. My customers like it when they're able to check out quickly, so tap and wallet are popular. And I get paid bonuses depending on customer reviews, so I always point out the link on their receipt and ask them to give me a 5."

There are a couple of learnings here. First, don't try to define a customer's job for them. Let the customer do that. Second, people are usually passionate about what they do. Sit down with them. Explain how your product helps them do their job, then let them tell it in their own words. Like this:

> "I work with customers, which are the lifeblood of our company. Great service is always my goal, and the new register helps me do just that. Customers love that I can easily find an item for them that might be missing on the shelves, give them the price, and either find it in the back room or ship it to their house from anywhere in the country. And it's fast. *Really* fast. They like the new tap and wallet payment features too."

Your messaging won't wither and die—it will come alive. You're going to take credit for the outcome anyway, but in a far more elegant fashion. Besides, the cut-and-paste messages already exist on your web page, in your case studies, your white papers, and all over your social media. A story is your opportunity to make it all real. To let your audience see how your product makes a difference. *When your objective is to tell a story, the essence of the message framed by the customer experience is far more powerful than the message itself.*

Now let's cover one final element that is integral to video storytelling.

## Music makes the world go round

Music is the third leg of the video storytelling stool—script, visuals, and music. If the music is weak, the story will be weak. If it's overpowering, it will be off balance. And if it doesn't match the style, it will simply be awkward or ugly.

The music should work in harmony with the script and visuals to form the complete picture. It shouldn't be an afterthought or chosen independent of the storyline. The music should reflect the tone of your video, and ebb and flow in step with the action. Sometimes a line in the script might be the first indication of an inflection point, sometimes there will be a visual cue, and sometimes a shift in the music can let the audience know that something is about to happen.

Music is *always* an integral part of the story. The Academy of Motion Picture Arts and Sciences knows this. That's why they give out awards for Best Original Score, Best Original Song, and Best Sound. Music can elevate the story, make it dull, or drown it out.

Be intentional about your music choice and its application. Avoid the repetitive, driving, overly electronic music tracks that are the mainstay of case studies and explainer videos. They're too harsh and monotonous to track a sensitive storyline. Watch the volume too. The music should support and enhance, but it should never become the center of attention.

And that brings the how-to part of the conversation to a close. You've learned how to select a cast and craft a storyline. You know the universal tricks of the trade, how to practice literary excellence, and how to up your video game. In Part 3, you will learn how to finish the job.

 **Fingertip reminders**

Before we go, here are a few final reminders on the mechanics of business storytelling.

- A messaging framework distills your product's strongest talking points into a cohesive narrative and gets everybody on the same page. But it's too product-centric, industry-specific, and salesy for a story.

- Canned corporate messages coming from the mouth of a customer sound contrived. Let customers make it relatable to their own experience and phrase it in their own words.

- Be intentional about your music choice and its application. It should support and enhance, but never become the center of attention.

# PART 3
## CROSS THE FINISH LINE

AND NOW IT'S time to put the final touches on your storytelling skills. Storyline mastery, literary excellence, and video savvy are necessities—but they don't guarantee success. You can be adept at creating a storyline but fail to get the customer on board. You can shoot a great video then have it destroyed during review cycles. You can write a great story and never have it see the light of day. There are scads of corporate pitfalls between you and the finish line.

In comparison, novelists and how-to authors seem to have it easy. They don't deal with the tug of war from product managers, keynote executives, legal departments, sales teams, web teams, and content quotas.

The biggest challenge to a corporate storyteller is simply learning to navigate these hurdles in order to master both the storytelling elements and the corporate maze. You will need to be adept at wearing a lot of hats to cross the finish line with a great story. So let's talk about the hats.

# COMMUNICATOR

COMMUNICATION SKILLS ARE a big deal. Every person you want to influence, every point you want to hammer home, and ultimately every story you want to produce will rely on your ability to communicate. Unfortunately, writing and speaking skills alone won't get you there. It's also about what you choose to say, when you choose to say it, and how you frame the conversation.

Years ago I was asked to improve the output from a Microsoft vendor. They were managing a case study program, and it wasn't going well. The reason didn't stay hidden for long. Once the vendor got ahold of my email address, they slapped me on the cc line of their copious email machine and filled my Inbox.

It seems the vendor measured progress by the quantity and verbosity of communications, instead of by quality of work. Each email was filled with unhelpful information, no clarifying instruction, and a looming deadline with the ball in my court. I was starting to wonder exactly what tasks were in the vendor's court, other than writing increasingly demanding emails.

Even when I took the time to wade through the content, often the information I actually needed wasn't in the email. It might have been in a previous email several steps back, or attached to a different email with a different subject line, or it might not exist at all. I started to question what value, if any, the vendor was contributing to the program.

It turned out, not much. After spending an inordinate amount of time meeting with the team face-to-face and trying to pin down exactly where we were on each project, it became clear that we were not on the precipice of case study success. Instead, customers were dropping out of projects. Some faded away, and others slammed the door shut. The remaining efforts were unimpressive and bogged down. The reason? The vendor's poor communication skills. The customers—some of whom were executives at high-visibility brands—weren't any better at decoding the long, confusing emails than I was! Bad communication was torpedoing the team's efforts while damaging important customer relationships.

## Winning maneuvers

Granted, the example above was about case studies, but the same principles hold true for any kind of communication. And they're integral to your storytelling success. Let's take a closer look.

Good business communications have the following qualities: they're necessary, consolidated, respectful, concise, comprehensive, clear, and sent via the recipient's preferred channel. Now we'll piece that out.

### *Necessary*

If a person won't find your communication useful, don't send it to them. Think of the dreaded "Reply All" some folks use in response to every "Welcome to our giant company!" email. People get angry about these things. They don't want their Inbox filled with irrelevant information. Not only have you wasted their time, but you've left an impression. And it's not a good one.

The same is true for the communications attached to a storytelling project. Scan every distribution list. Don't leave anyone off that should be included, and don't include anyone who should be left off. Both rules are important.

Then make sure your communication is tight. No one wants to read a rambling mess. Include the information that people need to know and ditch everything else.

### Consolidated

Make it easy for your recipient by consolidating communications. If you have sent seven emails asking for their input on various topics, don't send seven more emails asking them to respond. Send one. The investment in time will pay big dividends.

It's easy. Just create an appropriate subject line such as "Consolidating requests" and begin the email by clearly stating the purpose, then line up all of the items that need their attention. Be sure to include everything they need to quickly capture the context and create a response. Like this:

Hi Jenn,

I hope your trip to New York went well. We have several moving parts across multiple projects right now, so I've consolidated everything for you below. Feel free to disregard previous requests.

- Attached is a draft of the storyline for the manufacturing video. The customer is on board. **Any concerns?**

- Also attached is a draft email to the customer requesting they participate in the keynote at

ManufacturingEurope. **Would you kindly open and
hit "Send"?**

- The final video for the energy story is ready for **your
approval <u>here</u>.**

- Julia would like video options to open the
panel discussion on Day Two of next month's
RetailSuperEvent. **Okay to send Percolator and
PantOriginals videos?**

Be sure to include adequate context, attach relevant files,
and bold the questions you want them to answer. Keep it short,
but comprehensive.

The same approach works for customers and end users.
For example, if you want a customer to commit to a shoot
schedule, provide the proper contact for building access,
and co-present at an event—send it all in one email. Keep
it short, formulate the questions so they're easy to answer,
and give them all the information they need to evaluate and
respond.

### *Respectful*

Watch your tone. Remember to enter the conversation
with a gracious comment, but don't belabor the niceties. Be
friendly, but not *too* friendly. Follow the recipient's lead on
familiarity—some people prefer formal work relationships;
others are more open. Respond appropriately, but never
become overly familiar with a client. It's best to remain *slightly*
more formal than your customer and always within respectful
guidelines.

## Concise

Learn to revere brevity. Your audience will love you for it. It takes considerably more time to write a compact email than a long one, but take the time anyway.

Long-winded emails are often a sign that you haven't done your homework. That you haven't spent enough time or learned your topic well enough to be concise, and so you ramble. Writing *more* won't fool anyone into thinking you know what you're talking about—and it's likely to do the opposite.

Make sure you know your business well enough to state it succinctly before you write an email. The same is true for a phone call or an in-person meeting; take the time to be prepared. Not only are short communications more efficient, they're a matter of courtesy. Remember, people are fighting through their Inbox hoping to wrap things up and be done for the day. They may be looking forward to a dinner date or hoping to catch their child's baseball game. Don't be the reason they miss it.

## Comprehensive and clear

Brief is great. But you also need to be so well-versed on the issue that you can explain it both briefly *and* precisely. An economy of words won't release you from the need to be comprehensive and clear.

Ensure that all of the relevant material is at your recipient's fingertips: if you are referring to a document, attach it. If you want them to review a video, link it. If you are asking someone to make a request by email, include the contact information and title. Better yet—draft the email yourself and then attach it to your email request. People will love you for it.

At the opposite end of the spectrum, *never* send an email that requires the recipient to hunt down information or dig for a previous email in order to respond. No one wants a homework assignment. Ideally, your communication is so clear and so complete that they can assimilate and respond immediately. Best case, they won't even have follow-up questions.

And beware the curse of assumed knowledge. Once you become deeply familiar with a subject, it can start to feel like universal wisdom. Surely everyone already knows what you're talking about, so you leave off important information. Instead of providing context, you start in the middle. But if you don't bring the audience up to speed, they may feel as if they've just walked into the theatre halfway through a movie. They're lost.

So take a different approach. Start by laying the groundwork. Be thorough but brief. Hit every key point that is relevant to the conversation and skip everything else. Keep it compact. Concise. Succinct. Whatever descriptor works for you.

### Preferred channel

And finally, customize the channel for each recipient. Some people are great with email. Others prefer text, or phone, or in corporate settings, a chat app like Slack or Teams. Think about which channel is most likely to reach your audience and how you might maximize the chances they will respond. Here's how that might play out.

A few years ago I worked on a video for a healthcare company. I'd convinced the product manager that the story would be stronger with an end user, so he dug up the name of a patient whose story was interesting. Neither of us knew the patient, but the product manager was privy to the contact information and I wasn't. He insisted on reaching out himself.

The project dragged out for weeks. Then months. The patient simply didn't respond. I asked politely for the contact info. I reminded him gently. I begged. I pleaded. We went through several rounds of promises: "If he doesn't respond this time, I'll give you his phone and email."

Then the product manager left the company. It was a turning point for the story. I met with his replacement right away, explained the situation, and asked for the contact information. She gave it to me the same day, and within 48 hours the patient had agreed to participate and I had the release form in my hand.

What was the difference? The first product manager had emailed the patient with a formal, businesslike request. Multiple times. With a legal release attached. Instead, I called his cell phone and left a friendly message, then waited one day and sent a polite text. He called me right back, and when I told him what I wanted he was all-in.

The patient was excited. He *wanted* to tell his story. So why hadn't he responded before? He didn't like email. It was too "official-sounding," he couldn't quite tell what was required of him, and there wasn't opportunity for real-time questions. And he found the attached legal release more than a little off-putting.

Once we were able to talk and I answered all of his questions, he was ready to sign—but there was one final obstacle. The email had instructed the patient to sign the release form and return it by Federal Express, but that method didn't work for him. The patient lived in a small, rural Midwest town. The closest FedEx store was 35 minutes away—and the last thing he wanted to do after work was to spend over an hour running an errand in the opposite direction of his house.

But he told me he could fax the form from work. Would that be okay? I assured him that whatever was easiest for him would be great. Then I scrambled to hook up the fax service on my home office printer and we were done. Bam. And his story was amazing.

Your communication skills will have a huge impact on your ability to tell great stories. Before you dial, schedule a meeting, or send an email ask yourself: is this communication necessary? Have I consolidated everything and made it easy for them to assimilate and respond? Have I set the stage with the right amount of context, but kept it succinct? Is my message clear? Is the tone respectful? And have I chosen the channel that works best for the recipient?

### Final check

We're all moving fast and sometimes that means mistakes. Communications are important, so take the time to check your work. You may *think* you've provided all the background and filled in all the blanks—but you haven't. What was in your mind did not come out of your mouth, even though you intended it to.

Have you ever written something incorrectly and then repeatedly overlooked the mistake when you reread it? We all tend to read what we *think* we've written, even if it's incorrect or missing completely. Our minds fill in the blanks, and it makes perfect sense to us. But not to our audience.

There are two tricks you can use to make sure you've included everything. First, read it out loud—or under your breath if you're worried about distracting other people. You're far less likely to interject a word that doesn't exist if you engage your vocal cords.

Second, work from a mental or literal check list: Did I include these items? Where's the link? What about the attachment?

Then methodically verify that each item on the list is actually in the communication.

 **Fingertip reminders**

Every person you want to influence, every point you want to hammer home, and ultimately every story you want to produce will rely on your ability to communicate.

Here are a few tips to improve your communication:

- Necessary – If a person won't find your communication useful, don't send it to them.

- Respectful – Follow the recipient's lead on familiarity.

- Concise – Know your business well enough to state it concisely.

- Comprehensive – Ensure that all of the relevant material is at your recipient's fingertips.

- Clear – Briefly lay the groundwork and hit every key point that is relevant.

- Preferred channel – Customize the channel to the recipient.

- Final check – take the time to review your work. Did it meet the mark?

# SALESPERSON

I F YOU WANT to be a great business storyteller, keep your eye on the ball. Remember *why* you're telling stories: to help the sales team sell. Yes, stories are inspirational. They make a human connection. They'll capture more attention than a case study. But why are you creating content in the first place? It's to sell more stuff.

You need to clear two big hurdles in the sales department. First, ensuring that the content you create has real sales value. And second, honing your own sales skills in order to shove that content across the finish line.

## The right content

What's the best way to know what type of content the sales team needs? Ask them. I surveyed salespeople in two Fortune 100 companies and asked them to rate the usefulness of various types of content. In each survey fewer than 80% felt case studies were a useful sales tool, while over 90% rated stories as useful.

So why—when salespeople rank stories more than 10 points higher than case studies—do marketing departments continue to lag in creating authentic stories? Chances are they either don't know the difference, or it's too doggone hard to shove stories across the finish line.

But you don't have the first problem—you already know the difference between a case study and a story. Now you just need to tackle the second problem by developing your own sales skills.

## The fine art of finesse

Business storytelling requires a lot of relationship-building, an abundance of hand-holding, a clever eye to process, and a heavy dose of emotional wisdom. What makes your stakeholders tick? And how can you use that information to inch your story closer to the finish line?

Sometimes stakeholders are eager to help, sometimes not. Sometimes they need more information, sometimes less. Sometimes the deadline needs pulled up, sometimes pushed back. Shoving new stories over the finish line means managing the needs of every single person between your story and final publication. And sometimes that's a long list. But with a little practice, you can learn to win over most of the stakeholders most of the time. I call it the fine art of finesse. Real salespeople call it sales.

The trick is to put yourself in the shoes of every person you need on your team. Figure out what their concern is, then address it.

Here are a few examples of who might be on your list and what might be important to them.

| STAKEHOLDER | PRIMARY CONCERN |
|---|---|
| Salesperson | Protect customer relationships and sell more stuff |
| Customer | Sell their own stuff |

| STAKEHOLDER | PRIMARY CONCERN |
| --- | --- |
| Product Manager | Present the product accurately and showcase differentiated features |
| Marketing | Ensure content is on-message and meets the needs of a wide variety of asks |
| Public Relations | Up-level content that shows the company in a positive light |
| Executive | Snag new, compelling content to debut at major events and with high-profile customers |

Now let's pick one person and see if we can address their concerns. Actually, we'll pick two—because the salesperson and customer are inextricably linked.

The salesperson has plenty of reason to be leery of your request. They've probably spent months or even years building a network of hard-won relationships—and they won't be eager to put them at risk. After all, relationships drive sales, and sales determine the size of their paycheck and the status of their job security. It's doubtful they'll just hand you the contact information and head on down the road. First, you need to show them that you can be trusted with their most important resource. Second, you need to collect the background you'll need for the customer call.

We'll start with the trust issue. In sales, time is money and relationships are king. Any request for their help should be a succinct missive that addresses their concerns. Plan your conversation ahead of time.

Start with these promises:

- You will handle the customer with care.
- You will position the customer as the hero of the story and work collaboratively with them on the storyline.
- You will do your absolute best to make sure the customer is super happy with the process and with the results.
- You will follow the salesperson's lead on how much they want to be included in phone calls, copied on correspondence, and updated on progress.

And include these fact-finding questions:

- What is the current state of the customer relationship and any imminent or ongoing deals?
- How much progress have they made in adopting the new product or service?
- Tell me about the customer experience. Any significant wins (or losses) to-date?
- Who will you be speaking with, what is their position in the company, and are there any useful tidbits you should know?

Once the salesperson is on board, ask them to include you in an email to the customer. Let's assume you want the customer to participate in a video: the first goal is simply to get the customer to say "yes" to a brief phone call. This is a "let's talk about the opportunity" call, and all you want from the salesperson is their help to get the customer on the phone. That's it.

The salesperson is welcome to attend the call, but don't make them the middleman. If they offer to present the opportunity, don't take them up on it. If they press, talk them out of it. Chances are you will lose the opportunity if the salesperson takes the lead, not because they can't manage a customer conversation (they're experts at it), but because they're not equipped for *this* conversation. The salesperson won't know the process well enough—or your ability to flex—to present the opportunity well. They also won't be familiar enough with how your video crew operates in order to address all those hidden objections that may be between you and a story.

Be prepared to address the customer's risk too. You want to offer lots of upside, no cost, and low risk. Remember that their primary allegiance is to *their* brand, not yours. The customer conversation is all about the customer, nothing else. Use words like partnership, collaboration, and appreciation.

And don't shove a legal release in their face. If you do, most of the customers you *really* want to land will say "no." Many times they won't even take your call. And to top it all off, the salesperson isn't likely to provide an introduction the next time you're looking for help.

Instead, frame the customer conversation as an opportunity— then make sure you come through. The customer will help you tell your story; you will make them shine.

The initial phone conversation may go something like this:

"We'll agree on the topics ahead of time so there are no surprises. My favorite video crew is all lined up for the shoot. I've worked with them in all kinds of situations all over the world and they are excellent. They are highly professional, have shot in all kinds of situations, and will follow your lead on any business or security issues. I'll be there too, and will be watching to make sure everything goes smoothly. The interview is super low pressure, it's more like an informal conversation. The director will sit down with you and ask you a bunch of questions. If you mess up 16 times, we'll just shoot it 17 times. No problem. Folks always say how much fun they had during the shoot and how pleased they are with the results. Once we have a video cut, we'll send it past you for final approval before it becomes public, and we're glad to give you a copy of the final file for your own marketing purposes."

By the end of the conversation, the customer should not feel as if they're doing *you* a favor; in fact, they should feel as if you're doing *them* a favor. Your goal is to make them *want* to participate. To be part of a video that positions their brand as the hero—and that they can use in their own marketing— without spending any of their own budget! Lots of upside, no cost, low risk.

The proper time to ask for the release form is *after* they've bought in. Asking for the release at the beginning of the process is the goofiest move I've ever seen. It's like walking onto a car lot and having a salesperson shove a contract in your face—before you've even decided if you want to buy a car! The customer will sign the release form when they're comfortable with the decision. It's your job to make them comfortable.

Once they show interest, be sure to mention on the phone call (never by email) that you won't be able to publish the story without their written consent. Again, this is for *their* benefit. Let them know that you will send a document their way for signature.

And never call it a "legal release." Find the least one-sided, overbearing document that has the blessing of your legal team, rename it "release form," and send it in a follow-up email right after the first phone call. It's always nice to get a signature before you invest in a phone interview, but don't be surprised if it doesn't happen that way. The customer may need to feel out the process, experience the interview, and gain insight into the storyline before they're willing to sign on.

If your customer is also the end user, then you're done with the casting call. If not, you have another sales job ahead of you to convince your main character to sign on. No matter where you are in the process, figure out what makes each stakeholder tick and help them meet their goals. Make it easy to say "yes" and hard to say "no." Now we're going to move on to the next step, but remember to keep selling throughout the process.

 **Fingertip reminders**

The overarching reason for content creation is to sell more stuff. Stories give you a unique opportunity to do that.

Here are a couple of tips:

- The right content – Salespeople rank stories more than 10 points higher than case studies.

- The fine art of finesse – Business storytelling requires a lot of relationship-building, an abundance of hand-holding, a clever eye to process, and a heavy dose of emotional wisdom.

And here are some examples of stakeholders and what might be important to them:

| STAKEHOLDER | PRIMARY CONCERN |
|---|---|
| Salesperson | Protect customer relationships and sell more stuff |
| Customer | Sell their own stuff |

| STAKEHOLDER | PRIMARY CONCERN |
| --- | --- |
| Product Manager | Present the product accurately and showcase differentiated features |
| Marketing | Ensure content is on-message and meets the needs of a wide variety of asks |
| Public Relations | Up-level content that shows the company in a positive light |
| Executive | Snag new, compelling content to debut at major events and with high-profile customers |

# INTERVIEWER

ONCE YOUR CAST of characters has signed on, it's time to flesh out your storyline via interviews with each character. You're looking for both the background (the information) and the human element (the inspiration).

## Gather the information

Gathering the background information is easy. You simply need to be gracious and ask the right questions.

Here are a few pointers to get you started:

- Learn about the customer relationship and their experience with the product ahead of time.

- Design good questions to help you verify details and uncover any missing information.

- Take the time to build rapport and be courteous.

- Listen carefully and ask good follow-up questions.

- Record the call.

When you do the interview, be pleasant. Thank them for their time. Form an authentic relationship but keep it at an appropriate level. Don't be creepy. No need to invite them out for drinks or ask to see pictures of their kids.

I know it's listed above, but I can't stress this enough: *always* record interviews—after asking for permission of course. Not only is a recording the best source for brainstorming a storyline, but it frees you from note-taking so you can conduct a better interview. Just let your interviewee know the information won't be shared publicly and most folks will be fine with it. I've done hundreds of interviews and I've only had one person tell me no—and frankly they were an internal stakeholder without substantial input. Go figure.

One note on technology: it fails. A lot. So have a backup. I once had three people recording on three devices for an international story. Two of the recordings failed completely.

## Discover the inspiration

Now that you have the basics down, it's time to graduate to more advanced interview skills. The questions you ask in an interview are usually designed to get basic information, like how a product was used, when the customer started using it, and what results they saw. The answers to those questions will give you what you might need for a case study, but you're looking for more. You need to uncover a storyline. That involves listening carefully for clues that might lead to a great story. When you hear one, don't be afraid to veer off course and ask about it. That's how digging for a story works – you get the subject talking and sharing details until you hit paydirt. Here's an example:

Do you remember the guy who loved to fish? He had chronic kidney disease. During the interview—in amongst all the medical details—I asked him a question. What had his disease taken away from him? His answer was quick and decisive. Kidney disease had viciously stripped away the two things that brought him the most joy in life: providing for his family, and fishing. Thanks to a kidney transplant and renewed health, he had regained both.

Here was the inspiration we needed. The loss. The fear. The sorrow. The joy of recovery. This is where the storyline lived. Just below the surface.

We infused the patient's love and care for his family throughout the storyline, then used his love of fishing to fashion a meaningful bookend for the story. The video opened with a beautiful early morning scene. He was fishing in a small boat on a gorgeous country lake. He was relaxed. Happy.

The next scene showed his fishing gear neglected and dusty in the garage as he struggled with the weakness and fatigue of chronic kidney disease. We saw him toil to find a kidney donor, only to have someone back out. He nearly gave up.

Then the story turned. We felt his relief when he finally found a donor and was able to get a transplant. And finally, we experienced his joy as he pulled his fishing gear out of the garage, slung it onto his boat, and headed back to the lake. He was fishing by dawn.

It was a beautiful backdrop that answered the "so what?" question that is central to every story. Sure, the solution helped him manage his kidney disease, but so what? What is the value in human terms? For this patient, it was a second chance at life.

## Transcribe the transcript

Sometimes the conflict reveals itself clearly during the interview. Sometimes you will need to study the transcript and brainstorm options. In every case the transcript is invaluable, so arrange for the transcription as soon as the interview is over.

When I read through a transcript, I highlight three elements: awesome sound bites, phrases that support key messaging, and anything I think will help design a storyline. I mentally file the sound bites and messaging, then mull over the storyline options. I call in other creatives and we put our thinking caps on. In the end, we choose the most relatable conflict that will produce the steepest bend in the story arc. Then, we go to work filling in the details for an engaging and cohesive storyline.

Interviewing takes practice and skill, so study the pointers and start interviewing. You will improve and so will your stories. Next we'll explore the role of negotiator. But first, a few reminders.

 **Fingertip reminders**

Interviewing is a skill that will improve with practice. When you step out of the interview, you should have all of the background information and human inspiration you need to craft a storyline.

Here are a few interview tips:

- Learn about the product, customer, and deployment ahead of time.
- Design good questions to help you verify details and uncover any missing information.
- Take the time to build rapport and be courteous.
- Don't forget to listen and ask good follow-up questions.
- Record the call.

And follow this basic order:

- Gather the information.
- Discover the inspiration.
- Transcribe the transcript.

# NEGOTIATOR

**M**ARKETERS WANT TO see their carefully constructed messaging infused in the video script. Product teams want features and benefits. Salespeople want the story to be compelling enough to drive sales. Brand wants it to be engaging. Customers want to insert their own brand messaging. Executives want it to be inspiring enough to show in their next keynote. Legal wants it to be carefully vetted for anything that could be construed as a claim. It's like getting a room full of preschoolers to agree on a snack.

So what do you do? You negotiate in order to protect the storyline. You take extensive, clunky edits and refashion them into something more eloquent. You reword key messages into something a real person might actually say, and exchange "will" for "may" to make the lawyer happy.

It's a huge challenge, but it's *so* important. If you fail here, all of your hard work goes down the drain. Luckily, you can learn how to be a better negotiator with a winning game plan.

## Get everyone on the same page

If everyone's fuzzy on the end goal, the project will wander all over the place. So lay the groundwork early. Establish a firm objective for the project.

Here's what a goal might look like for an upcoming story:

"Show the impact of remote power management on the education, health, and opportunities for children living in the remote villages of Nigeria. The tone is human, memorable, and inspiring."

How often do you repeat the goal? Constantly. People are moving fast through their workday. What will they do when a customer story flies across their desk? They will do what they always do. Product managers will insert every possible feature and benefit. Marketers will cut and paste canned messages into the story. Customers will insert *their* canned messages. And on and on it goes, in a whirlwind of competing priorities—unless you keep everyone focused on the goal.

Attach the project goal to every request for input or approval. Measure against it. Use it as a shield to protect your story from the slings and arrows of bad feedback.

## Manage the feedback

You can avoid a lot of unpleasantness—and a shredded storyline—by managing the feedback cycles well. First, don't go backwards. Unless there's been a huge turn of events, there's no need to rehash why you're telling the story, or when there's going to be a story about Product X, or why the Northeast Sales District gets all the good stories. These are all good things to discuss, but their time has passed. That happened earlier. So remind them of the project goal and ask for their help.

Second, never throw out an open-ended request for input. If you do, you'll get open-ended feedback of any length and on any topic—including attempts at copy editing. It's human nature: ask for input and folks will oblige.

So watch the wording. Ask reviewers to focus on *where you have missed the mark*. Their role is to measure against the agreed-upon goal and point out any problems, especially any inaccuracies in product capabilities or customer experience. The story is human, but the solution underneath must be represented with impeccable accuracy. This is where reviewers can help.

Let's say you're creating a voiceover video script for the power management story in Nigeria. The approach for a voiceover script is completely different than an interview. Pre-written scripts have a dangerous propensity to lean toward stale marketing language, so couch your request carefully.

Here's how I might request feedback on the Nigeria story—after reminding everyone of the project goal:

> Thank you for your help with our upcoming power management story in Nigeria. Attached is the draft video script. Would you kindly review for any *inaccurate product details or misalignment with key messages?*

Third, ask reviewers to add comments rather than editing directly in a document. You don't want or need them to rewrite the story—you just want to know about anything that's technically incorrect. Of course, even if you ask for comments rather than direct edits, chances are they'll edit the document anyway. You can make your job easier by turning on "track changes" before you send the script for review. If (or when) that fails, you can use a "compare" feature to reveal the edits.

And finally, once you gather all of the feedback, apply it thoughtfully. Lots of people may have suggested (or made) changes to the story, but writing by committee is never a good idea. You need to look past the comments or edits to figure out what the reviewers are really trying to say, then incorporate their feedback in a way that maintains both style and storyline.

## The special case

Feedback from your legal team requires an especially delicate hand. Their job is to mitigate risk, and they're good at it. The problem is: risk mitigation may be valuable, but it's rarely eloquent. In fact, a legal review can decimate a great story in the blink of an eye. I swear there's a class on "story destruction" in every law school.

And lawyers have pull. They have the power to insist on some changes and strongly recommend others, so you'll need to negotiate. The lawyer wins on risk management; you win on phrasing. Look at all the angles. Work toward a balanced approach that mitigates risk while maintaining inspiration. Make it a point to understand any legal concerns, then leverage your writing skills to make smooth adjustments.

Here's an example. One time I was asked to help resolve legal feedback on a video script. I opened the document to find significant edits on 12 sentences out of 17. And 6 of the edits were long, clunky phrases—all added to what was supposed to be a 90-second video.

The lawyer had a point: he was trying to avoid any wording that could be construed as a promise or a claim. That's fair enough. Marketers will always lean toward sweeping generalizations; lawyers will always work to rein them in. Unfortunately, in his attempt to save the company from potential ruin, the lawyer had done a fair job of destroying the script.

So I countered. By analyzing *why* he was heavy-handed with

the red pen, I was able to negotiate a compromise. It turned out two nasty words had found their way into the early part of the script: "is" and "will." Those two little words made it sound like the entire script was promising results—and lawyers don't like to promise anything. Once that red pen was out, the ink kept flowing.

But I had a better idea: what if we simply scrubbed away those hideous words? I changed "is" to a softer "can be," and replaced "will" with "may." That's it. The lawyer was happy, the story was still engaging, and the marketing team was relieved.

The legal review is always nerve-wracking, but you can often avoid having a story shredded by lawyers with a little proactive attention to phraseology.

## Fuel for the fire

Let's imagine you're working on a story about self-driving vehicles. What do you think a legal team might say about this line?

"[Brand X] puts artificial intelligence behind the wheel. We pay attention to the road, so you don't have to."

Good luck getting that past a legal review. You're implying that your company takes responsibility for driving the vehicle—and any property damage, personal injury, or death resulting from it—and that the consumer doesn't need to pay attention. Not a good position.

How about this?

"Artificial intelligence from [Brand X] fuels the cars that drive themselves."

Better. It's catchier, and you're not encouraging the people in the car to play solitaire. Your legal team may still object though—to a lawyer, this could still put your brand in a position of responsibility for the car.

And what if you said this?

"Artificial intelligence from [Brand X] fuels the future of driving."

That might be just fuzzy enough. Only your legal team can make the call, but you get the idea. Don't waste your time on wording that is sure to be objectionable—because once that red pen comes out, it can be hard to get the cap back on.

Ideally, a proactive eye toward legal considerations will help your story sail through legal review. If you do get feedback, your job is to find a solution that resolves legal concerns while preserving the storyline. *Never* give up your obligation to the audience. Very few people enjoy reading legal jargon, and it's highly unlikely your audience will either.

## The other team

And while we're talking about lawyers, don't forget about the customer's legal team. I have found that problems typically show up early in the process—when the release form passes through their legal department. You're asking the customer to commit to a story that they don't own, so it can get a little dicey. Sometimes they make a reasonable request and you can accommodate. Sometimes they make an unreasonable request and the story is dead in the water.

One of the most problematic revisions I have seen is a requirement to notify the customer every time you use the asset. That's a nonstarter. Once the story is complete, tons of internal folks will get their hands on it. There's no way you can ensure that each and every person will contact the customer—or contact *you* to contact the customer—every time they want to use the story. It's impossible. The customer is asking your company to agree to something they can't possibly do. I would either get them to abandon the request or move on. Chances are your legal department will insist on it anyway.

One final warning: don't think you've gotten off scot-free if your customer *doesn't* send the release form for legal review. Once you send the asset for final approval, they will probably engage their legal department—which has just been blindsided because they didn't know there was a story in the works. It won't matter that you have a signature on the release form. If their legal department says "no," it's over.

It's a delicate dance for the storyteller. I don't insist customers run the release past their legal department—but I always offer to speak with them if they have questions or concerns. Typically just airing the topic is enough to ensure everyone is on board. And it keeps me from committing substantial dollars to a project that could die just short of the finish line.

## Final approval

Now that legal is on board, let's revisit the rest of the team. Once you've incorporated everyone's feedback, it's time for final approval. If you have followed the process, you're most of the way there. Everyone is already on board with the storyline, a real-life view of key messages, and the detailed plan. The final step should be easy. This is their opportunity to confirm that you did what you all agreed to do.

Here's how I might approach the customer for final video approval:

> "Thank you again for all of your help to create the video [insert link]. We are very pleased with the results and hope you are as well."

That's it. I've never had a customer fail to respond with their approval—even though I didn't explicitly ask—and I've never had a customer fail to say they love the video.

Notice I didn't say, "Take another look and see if you have any more changes." You've been down that road, and any additional edits you make based on one person's input will generate yet another approval cycle. If a legitimate issue somehow crept past everyone, of course you'll need to make the adjustment—just don't beg for input now. If you get everyone on the same page early, keep them updated throughout, and produce a knock-out piece of content, the final approval should sail right through.

 **Fingertip reminders**

If you want to protect the storyline—and you must—you need to learn to negotiate.

Here are some tips to help you on your way:

- Get everyone on the same page early by establishing a firm objective for the project.

- Manage feedback by pointing to the objective and asking for where you may have missed the mark. Never throw out an open-ended request for input.

- Pay special attention to legal issues. Protect the storyline while resolving all concerns.

- Consider the customer's legal team too. What actions should you take to ensure they're on board?

- Final approval should be a short email with a link to the final story and a note thanking the customer. Don't invite last-minute feedback by asking if there's anything else they want to change.

# PROJECT MANAGER

P ROJECT MANAGEMENT MAY sound dreary, but it needn't be. And it's so necessary. Good project management is what keeps everyone and everything on track. Without it deadlines slide, opportunities are missed, and people get grumpy.

If you're accountable for a deliverable, you're a project manager. Granted, sometimes the label is used loosely to describe the person who bugs everybody to review a piece of content by a certain date—but that's hardly project management. And any giant project will have a dedicated project manager—but that's not the rule for most content production. Still, every well-executed project has someone managing all of the elements needed to successfully shove it across the finish line.

Storytelling is no different. If you're responsible for the project, you need to nudge the story from Point A to Point B without letting it die in the process. And there are plenty of opportunities for a story to die: the timeline is too tight; the budget isn't adequate; key stakeholders can't agree on direction; market conditions aren't favorable; or it seems you can't get the right people on the bus. Project management skills are essential in order to juggle scope, time, cost, quality, stakeholder management, communications, and risk—all of which may be further complicated when vendors are involved.

Let's take a closer look. We've already talked about many of the elements that impact project success: scope (project goal), stakeholder management (sales and negotiation), risk (release forms and legal reviews), and communications (a must at every step). Now it's time to dig into three other elements: time, cost, and quality.

Have you ever seen one of those mobiles that infants love? You know—the kind where you can't touch the whale without sending the dolphin into a frenzy? Or the elephant and lion go into gyrations when you touch the zebra?

Mobiles have serious dependency issues. So do time, cost, and quality. You can't touch one without impacting the others. If you pull the deadline up too close, cost is likely to go up and quality may go down. If you insist on the very highest quality possible, time and cost may both go up. And if you demand the lowest possible cost, quality may take a hit and time may float to some distant date.

So what do you do? In my experience, it's best to fight for a generous budget at the onset, insist on excellent quality throughout, and work toward a deadline that doesn't endanger cost or quality. We'll pretend for a moment that you really have that kind of flexibility. How do you manage all of the moving parts so nothing falls through the cracks?

## Make it official

Sticky notes don't really work to manage a timeline. There are too many moving parts. Once your budget, delivery date, and quality bar are set, you need a tool to help manage all of those tasks and milestones between initiation and completion.

So what do you use? There are a ton of project management tools available, but many of them are too complicated to be practical. Who needs a Gannt chart for every piece of content? Some tools are so industry inbred they won't even render reports in an easily shareable format—which makes them essentially useless for this application.

What you really need for a simple project—and most content projects are simple—is a workback schedule. This is very different from the abbreviated list of milestones that is often labeled as a workback schedule and makes its rounds through email. A *real* workback schedule lists every task and assigns it a date. If one date slips, the workback schedule will instantly show any repercussions to the timeline. You can use any tool you like as long as you're able to capture all of the essential information: task, owner, due date, status, and whether it's a milestone or not.

Here's a spreadsheet showing just the Background phase for a fictitious story.

**Best Customer Story Ever**

| | | |
|---|---|---|
| **Today's Date:** | 6/18/20XX |
| **Deliverable Due:** | 9/3/20XX |
| **T-minus (days)** | 77 |
| **T-minus (weeks)** | 11.0 |
| **T-minus (months)** | 2.75 |

| Days Allocated | Due Date | Phase | Milestone | Task | Owner | Status |
|---|---|---|---|---|---|---|
| 5 | 27-Apr | Background | | Speak with product manager | Elaine | Complete |
| 5 | 2-May | Background | | Draft interview questions | Elaine | Complete |
| 3 | 5-May | Background | | Finalize questionnaires | Elaine | Complete |
| 4 | 9-May | Background | | Interview customer | Elaine | |
| 3 | 12-May | Background | | Interview end user | Elaine | |
| 4 | 16-May | Background | Yes | Complete transcripts | Jennifer | |

Notice that all of these tasks are dependent. I can't draft the interview questions until I speak with the product manager; I can't finalize the questionnaire until I've drafted the questions; and on down the line. In order to deal with the dependencies, I put in a simple formula that calculates each date based on the completion date of the previous task and tacks on however many days the next task will take.

So what happens if the product manager is on vacation for two weeks? The days you allocated to speak with the product manager just went from 5 to 19, and your timeline now looks like this:

**Best Customer Story Ever**

| | | |
|---|---|---|
| **Today's Date:** | 6/18/20XX |
| **Deliverable Due:** | 9/3/20XX |
| **T-minus (days)** | 77 |
| **T-minus (weeks)** | 11.0 |
| **T-minus (months)** | 2.75 |

| Days Allocated | Due Date | Phase | Milestone | Task | Owner | Status |
|---|---|---|---|---|---|---|
| 19 | 11-May | Background | | Speak with product manager | Elaine | Complete |
| 5 | 16-May | Background | | Draft interview questions | Elaine | Complete |
| 3 | 19-May | Background | | Finalize questionnaires | Elaine | Complete |
| 4 | 23-May | Background | | Interview customer | Elaine | |
| 3 | 26-May | Background | | Interview end user | Elaine | |
| 4 | 30-May | Background | Yes | Complete transcripts complete | Jennifer | |

Once the number of days changed on the first task, the due date for every subsequent task changed accordingly. You were planning to be done with the background interviews by May

16, but now it's going to be May 30. Notice, however, that the due date for the content didn't budge. You're going to need to make up the time somewhere.

There are ways to manage the cascading impact of time delays—find someone else to speak with, squeeze the days allocated to later tasks—but the workback schedule is instrumental in highlighting the situation. Once you know the impact, you can adjust.

And keep an eye on the milestones too. Here's a simple milestone view that's easy to capture and embed in a project update:

| Due Date | Task | Owner | Status |
|---|---|---|---|
| 30-May | Transcripts complete | Jennifer | **Complete** |
| 9-Jun | Storyline complete | Elaine | **Complete** |
| 14-Jun | Detailed plan complete | Elaine/Joe | **Complete** |
| 23-Jun | Video shoot complete | Miranda | |
| 7-Jul | Final video delivery | Elaine | |

With a bit of Excel wizardry you can create a template that is sortable every which way and will help keep you on track. If you're not an Excel wizard, you can get someone else to create a template for you. If Excel isn't your cup of tea, choose a different tool.

There are pros and cons to any project management tool, so choose one that works for you. For example, one tool might not account for weekends. Maybe you can make quick adjustments to fix that—or simply find a different tool that suits you better. Whatever you choose, make sure it's easy to snip relevant information and embed it in an email or slide.

## Bird's eye view

Now for some basic timeline guidance. Remember, all timelines are up in the air until release forms are signed. Assuming you're able to clear that hurdle, four to six weeks is usually reasonable to interview, draft, review, polish, and approve written copy.

Videos are far more complex and time-consuming. Eight to ten weeks is a reasonable estimate if everything goes smoothly. And don't forget the contingencies. If the customer can't find an interview time for three weeks—or the location isn't available in June—or reviewers don't respond in a timely fashion—it's going to take longer.

That's all well and good. Now what happens when you don't have the flexibility to choose the delivery date? How do you fill all of those content requirements on the corporate calendar?

## Pipeline management

Often the corporate calendar will dictate due dates. It's full of events, product announcements, and press opportunities—and everyone wants a great story to go along with their activity. The trouble is, great stories don't often ripen according to schedule. The best stories take months, and I've had some take over a year.

So what do you do? I suggest you get ahead of the curve by continually feeding and driving a pipeline so you have a better chance to pluck the right story out at the right time. The question is, how do you fill that pipeline? Begging rarely works, but incentives can if they're designed well—especially when you're incentivizing the sales team. Salespeople are coin operated. That's not an insult. It's a recognition that their paychecks are often tied to incentives. And they drive a pipeline.

Here's an example of an idea that *almost* worked. There was one little flaw. One of my clients decided to add customer story nominations to the scorecard for every salesperson. Unfortunately, there was no quality bar for nominations and no requirement that any of the customers actually participate in a story. The salespeople simply had to make nominations—so they did. We ended up with a lot of nominations, but very few stories.

The most successful method I have seen went straight to the customer. VIP customers were invited to join a program with enticing benefits, such as visibility into product roadmaps, invitations to exclusive events, access to executive staff, insight into new technologies, and hands-on deployment assistance. In return, the customers provided feedback on the products they deployed and agreed to participate in a customer story. The program not only pushed product development and adoption, but it succeeded in incubating several great stories.

 **Fingertip reminders**

Good project management is essential for storytelling success. Without it deadlines slide, opportunities are missed, and partnerships dissolve.

Here are a few notes to keep in mind:

- If you're accountable for a deliverable, you're a project manager.

- Time, cost, and quality are inextricably linked.

- Sticky notes won't work to manage a timeline. Find a simple tool that works for you and is easy to use for project updates.

Here's an example of a milestone view from an Excel spreadsheet:

| Due Date | Task | Owner | Status |
|----------|------|-------|--------|
| 30-May | Transcripts complete | Jennifer | **Complete** |
| 9-Jun | Storyline complete | Elaine | **Complete** |
| 14-Jun | Detailed plan complete | Elaine/Joe | **Complete** |
| 23-Jun | Video shoot complete | Miranda | |
| 7-Jul | Final video delivery | Elaine | |

- All timelines are up in the air until release forms are signed.
- Build flexibility into your timeline so you can adjust for the inevitable snags.
- Find a reliable way to feed your story pipeline.

# CONTENT STRATEGIST

O FTEN CONTENT STRATEGY is about determining what content should live where. But in my opinion, a knockout story belongs everywhere. Imagine that a story has just garnered a lot of attention on one platform—chances are it will add value to another. And once people see it, you will get requests for additional files. So be ready. Every good story deserves a portfolio, including an impact slide, still photos, and a social snip.

## Video files

Let's assume you just produced an amazing video. What do you do now? First, grab the right files. I always keep at least two video files on hand. First, the highest resolution possible that is widely playable on most any computer. You can always compress a video into a smaller file, but you can't go the other direction. I default to the highest resolution MP4 file. I've found it will work most anywhere including YouTube, websites, and any modern version of PowerPoint.

Second, insist on a copy of whatever file the editor is manipulating with their specialty editing software—even if you don't have the software to play it. Fair warning: the file will be huge. But it's worth the storage space for two reasons: you will have what you need for an event, and you can recut the video as needed in the future.

Often event producers will request both types of files: an MP4 to play in a booth or breakout room, and a native file such as an MOV for a large keynote stage. The native file (you may hear it called codec) provides more flexibility to do things like mix the music and voiceover tracks separately. Once the video is rendered into a more universally playable format like an MP4, the mix is baked in—which is why you will also want the native file for any future recuts.

## Social and photography

Now let's talk about what else you'll need. Be sure to create at least one cutdown to use on social media; 6-15 seconds is a good goal. You'll want static photos too. If you're shooting a high-profile video, shell out the extra money for an on-site photographer. If you haven't hired a photographer you can ask the video editor to pull static shots from the video, but the results won't be as crisp. Video *always* has motion, so some of your favorite shots may not be sharp enough for a photo.

Ask for the highest possible resolution. TIF files are great. If you ask for a PNG or JPG, it may be too small to use. And while you're at it, make sure you have an accurate final transcript. And finally, ask your agency to provide a TXT file for subtitles. Accessibility standards and compliance requirements have seen explosive growth over the past few years, so make sure you throw the appropriate files in your grab bag.

Okay, now you have all the video assets you may need. What other assets might be useful?

## Written copy

In my opinion, if your story is worthy of video budget you should start there. And once you have an amazing video, there's little reason to retell it in written form. However, there *is* value in creating an ancillary case study. This will give you two valuable assets: a knockout video that can land most anywhere, and a solid case study to swing the purchase decision in your direction.

But sometimes you might not shoot a video. In that case, you will have to choose. Either you can write two pieces—a human story and a case study—or choose between the two. Just remember to avoid the hammerdrill. A single piece of content cannot adequately perform as both a story and a case study, because *you cannot prioritize both information and inspiration in the same piece of content.* Besides, stories and case studies have different structural forms and speak to different audiences—so you have to choose a flavor.

## Impact slides

Now that you've created an amazing video and an impressive case study, which asset do you think the sales team will find most valuable? Neither. After all that work, it's the impact slide that salespeople rank #1. Salespeople, execs, and presenters routinely default to a presentation as their primary asset. They walk into the room—or onto a stage—with a slide deck. Your job is to get your stories into that deck.

If you want your stories to be used, create a clean, professional, and highly visual slide template and use it to distill each story you create. Then hand the salesperson or executive a polished deck filled with amazing stories. They may use the deck as-is, or they may excerpt stories and convert the style to match another deck, but they'll find it valuable either way. And be sure to embed the video on a separate slide and put it on auto-play. When the presenter hits next, the video will come to life.

Next we'll talk about the largest corporate content-consuming beast: the event. But first, here are a few reminders.

 **Fingertip reminders**

Often content strategy is all about determining what content should live where. But when you have a dynamite story, it's usable everywhere.

Here are a few tips to help you expand your story's reach:

- Every good story deserves a portfolio. Include an impact slide, still photos, and a social snip.

- Know what video files your web team, social team, and event team need and capture them all in a repository. Then add the native file for events and future recuts.

- You cannot prioritize both information and inspiration in the same piece of content, so you have to choose a flavor. Either you write an amazing customer story sans video, or you create a knockout video and an ancillary case study.

# KEYNOTE CONSULTANT

E VENTS OFFER A unique platform for visibility: a captive audience, executive engagement, media attention, and a large, well-lit stage. It's an ideal but largely untapped opportunity for storytelling.

Corporate events tend to be predictable. There's the eye-catching, ear-ringing opener with a big reveal showcasing the largest known talent the budget can afford. Then comes the keynote with the biggest and best executives headlining the open and close. Custom-designed slides march across the screen. Demos showcase key product announcements. Industry experts show up with more slides. Breakout sessions are designed by industry track for deeper dives on a variety of topics. There are booths, meals, and evening events. And everywhere, more slides.

Events are time-consuming, budget-swallowing adventures in marketing. Creating enough content to feed the event-beast is a huge undertaking. The easiest way to fill the cavernous time slots is to repackage the exact same messages from the latest framework or product promo into the voice of whichever executive is reading the talk track, and voilà! Add a snazzy deck and you're done.

There are other benefits to this approach. The product marketers have already approved the language, legal has already bought in, and the execs know the lingo. Unfortunately, in the midst of educating and informing the audience with the latest messaging, you miss the chance to give them a reason to care. A well-told story is your best shot at breaking through the monotony.

Events offer an amazing opportunity to put your best storytelling foot forward. Great stories have the power to cast vision, sway impressions, and forge partnerships. All of the content doesn't need to be in a storytelling format, but key moments should be. Beyond the slide decks and talking heads, stories offer a more engaging way to capture and inspire an audience. To leave them with memories instead of memorabilia. Inspiration rather than information. It's a mold-breaking opportunity for creativity that can deepen audience engagement and build brand excitement.

## Showcase the showstoppers

When you have a great story, give it a great platform. Here's an example. One of my clients offered a cloud-based glucose monitoring service, and one of the use cases was blood sugar management in pregnancy. High blood sugar kills unborn babies, so I dug around for a story. In the end, we were able to shoot a compelling video of a high-risk patient with pre-existing diabetes who had already lost five IVF babies and desperately wanted to keep her unborn twins. The closing shots with tiny baby feet and sweet smiles said it all: the service provided by the health care company mattered. It changed lives.

That video was finalized a few months before an upcoming event, so we held its publication in order to debut it in a keynote. When the video came to life, all the dreariness of features and benefits, messaging, and insider language went out the window.

In its place? A story of triumph over despair—and an indelible image of giggling, healthy twin babies. It was human, and it was a hit.

But we didn't stop there. I contacted the physician ahead of time and asked if she would be willing to participate in the event. We already knew she was knowledgeable, well-spoken, and comfortable on camera. She was also a fan of the service because it helped her take better care of her patients.

So when the video wrapped, the physician walked onto the stage. Now we were able to connect the human story to the life-saving service. Medical detail? No problem. Product value? Absolutely. The feedback from attendees was overwhelming— we had touched a nerve. We weren't just showing them the value of a product—we were reminding them why their work matters.

## Detach from the demos

Sometimes you might have an awesome video, but the keynote calls for an on-stage demo to serve the needs of a technical audience. The problem is—nobody wants to see the features displayed in a video prior to a live, in-depth, on-stage demo. If you don't want your story cut from the program and relegated to a web page, there's a simple solution: cut the product detail from the video.

Remember the Nigeria story? The one where reliable solar energy powered schools and clinics? Despite being a great video, it would not have found its way to an event stage in its final form because the product was revealed in the video. That was a problem for the follow-up demo.

So I recut the video. We created a 75-second event cut that showed *only* the human side of the story—the impact of life-saving vaccines and well-lit schools. We saw people able to receive a vaccine because the refrigerator at the clinic worked. And children able to read and work on computers because of reliable power. The strategy worked. Now the CEO could use the video to show the human impact of the product and then segue into the demo. We released the full video immediately following the keynote.

## Try something new

Never confine yourself to what has been done. There are tons of creative ways to bring a story to life besides a traditional video. I've hired talent to act out a story on-stage. I've taken a video and muted the voiceover so the emcee could tell the story live. I've used video to show the audience what it's like to look through the eyes of a person with macular degeneration—visual distortion and all.

One word of caution: you have to get your ideas past the event agency. Events are a high risk environment and you have one chance to get it right. There's no opportunity to go back and try again, and the event agency's reputation is on the line. They may push for the lowest risk scenario—which is typically what they've done a thousand times before.

So figure out how you can minimize the risk for the agency and have it all work within the confines of the event. If you can deliver your creativity in a standard video file where all they have to do is push play, they're going to be happy. If you try to push outside the typical event boundaries, you will need to put your new risk management and negotiation skills to work. But it will be worth it.

And now, another word of caution.

## What *not* to do

Have you ever read a piece that poses as a story but overlays a traditional marketing pitch? Events are prime territory for confusing the two. The room is full, the audience is attentive, and someone in the decision chain just can't resist—so key messages and product benefits get inserted into the story. I call the effect "resurfacing"—and it's deadly.

Imagine your goal is to lead your audience toward a treasure 30 feet underwater. This is the climax of the story and you need to draw them along as you go deeper, deeper, deeper . . . until they become so immersed in the plot that they're invested in the outcome. They care what happens to the hero.

Now what happens if an obvious marketing message interrupts the journey? The spell is broken, the audience floats back to the surface, and you have to work twice as hard to reengage them all over again—usually with limited success. Instead of taking the audience on a 30 foot journey into the depths of the story, they get 5 feet down and you bring them back to the surface. Over and over again. They end up taking 6 frustrating 5-foot journeys to nowhere. Although they've traveled the same distance, they haven't made any real progress. They bob along at the surface, never fully engaged and never reaching the depths where the story lives.

To realize the power of storytelling, give the messaging a spot to live outside of the story. You have plenty of opportunity. A single event may be strewn across at least one large keynote auditorium, several smaller presentation rooms, a plethora of workshops, and a hall filled with demo stations. Most of that content is a rotating carousel of features and benefits decorated with the latest messaging. Leave the story alone.

**Fingertip reminders**

Events offer a unique platform for visibility: a captive audience, executive engagement, media attention, and a large, well-lit stage. It's an ideal but largely untapped opportunity for storytelling.

Here are a few tips on how to incorporate storytelling into your next event:

- Showcase the showstoppers – Hold your most human videos for a keynote debut. If possible, follow it up with someone from the video.

- Detach from the demos – Create a special event cut that shows *only* the human side of the story. Leave the product information for the demo.

- Try something new – Explore new ways to tell a story outside of video or presentation. Ideas might include a stage play or a live video script delivery.

- What *not* to do – Don't mix messaging and storytelling. Let the story stand on its own.

# THE BIG PICTURE

B Y NOW I hope you have gained helpful insight into how business storytelling differs from mainstream storytelling. The age-old advice that works for novelists and how-to authors doesn't translate well to the business world. Novelists simply want to tell a story—business storytellers want to sell a product. Novels and memoirs are available on Amazon or in bookstores—business stories land on web pages, in customer visits, and at events. Novels and movies are typically lengthy adventures—business videos value brevity. The list of differences is long.

And that's not all. The complexity of the business world demands a broad set of skills simply to navigate the system. Let's take a final look at what it takes to cross the finish line, then we'll step back for a bird's eye view of everything we've learned.

 **Fingertip reminders**

Here's a list of hats that a great business storyteller must wear:

- Communicator – Every person you want to influence, every point you want to hammer home, and ultimately every story you want to produce will rely on your ability to communicate.

- Salesperson – Remember why you're telling stories: to help the sales team sell more stuff. You'll need some finely tuned sales skills to get everyone on board.

- Interviewer – Follow the side trails to uncover a storyline.

- Negotiator – Learn to negotiate past competing priorities in order to protect the storyline.

- Project manager – If you're accountable for a deliverable, you're a project manager.

- Content strategist – A good story belongs everywhere and in every form: video, written, social, photography. Just remember not to mix information and inspiration.

- Keynote consultant – Events are an ideal but largely untapped opportunity for storytelling.

## The final close

So that's it. We've done it. Business storytelling has been uniquely defined.

- Purpose – Inspiration
- Audience – Everyone
- Structure – Story arc

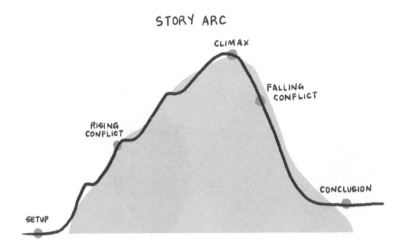

We've learned how to evaluate whether a story has the potential to land with impact.

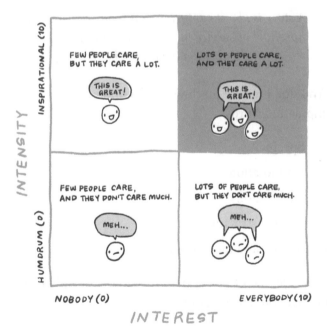

And put a stake in the ground on weighting characters.

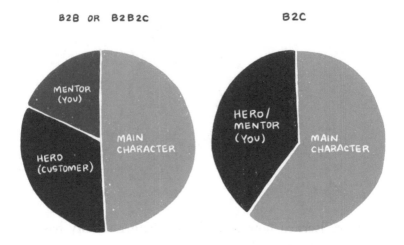

We've learned to recognize a story:

> *A story is about capturing that moment when your product or service intersects with humanity and changes a life for the better.*

And dug into the mechanics of writing to become better at manipulating words.

- Specificity
- Connotation
- Alliteration
- Parallel structure
- Similes and metaphors

We've learned to be better videographers and created a list to measure our story against.

- Compelling characters
- Engaging
- Captivating
- Surprising
- Memorable
- Inspiring
- Emotive opener
- Sticky middle
- Memorable close

On top of all that, we've explored the unique business skills needed to shove those stories across the finish line.

- Communicator
- Salesperson
- Interviewer
- Negotiator
- Project manager
- Content strategist
- Keynote consultant

So now what?

# WHERE DO YOU GO FROM HERE?

ASK YOURSELF THIS: Has the storytelling buzz been worth all the hoopla? Or have you eagerly anticipated its promises only to be disappointed by lackluster results? If so, you're not alone. The marketing world is in a rut. We've become expert hand crankers. Unfortunately, we've also become boring—and boring is not a great quality for a brand.

But if you're in a needle-moving mindset, this is your opportunity. It's time to dust off those storytelling shoes and try some new steps. Forget those pesky tweaks to well-worn molds—they're well-intentioned but misinformed. Start by learning to recognize what a story actually looks like and when to use it. Practice crafting a compelling storyline, then polish the techniques that will make your story come alive. Tackle all the skills you will need to navigate the corporate maze, then learn how to shove your story across the finish line—intact.

Once you battle your way through and create a new story— or two, or three—the conversation will become easier. And when your organization realizes the power of storytelling to captivate and inspire an audience, you will have a toe in the door.

You will know you're on your way when your stories begin to land on main web pages and high-visibility keynotes. New doors will open, with more opportunities to practice your storytelling skills across different products and customers.

Keep creating and the vision will grow. And always be willing to expand the circle of storytellers. Bring a novice storyteller along with you on your next project and teach them what works for you. Then encourage them to try it on their own. The business world is far from having too many good storytellers. Besides, creativity breeds creativity—and you can't have too much creativity in a marketing organization.

And finally, when you create a story you're excited about, send it to MyNewStory@GreatStories.com. I'm always up for hearing a great story.

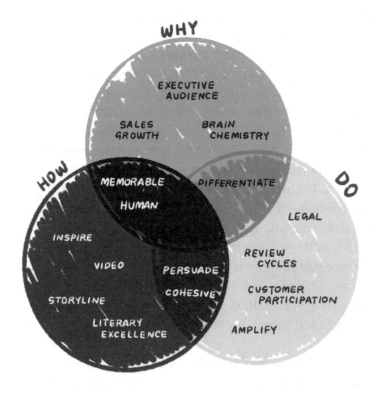

# ACKNOWLEDGMENTS

I DIDN'T SET OUT to write a book—it wasn't even on my radar—but as the years rolled by the decision made itself. The persistent appetite for great business stories simply refused to go away, yet there was little prescriptive advice on how to be a successful storyteller. So here we are. And I have so many people to thank—but I'll try to keep it short.

I must start with a personal thank you to my family who gave me nothing but encouragement despite the ridiculously long process of ideation, writing, rewriting, polishing, and publishing a book. I'm sure they wondered if I would ever get there—and if it would be worth reading if I did—but it never came out of their mouths. Bill, Alison, Greg, Jon, Kaley, Jackson, and Whitney, you are the world's finest cheerleaders.

My friend Adam Finley is the best book editor on the planet. (I realize I have absolutely no one to compare him to, but I stick by the statement.) He managed to work with a complete novice and give guidance that was accurate yet not destructive. He pulled me off of weird tangents, helped me see where things didn't flow, and encouraged me to find my own voice. His feedback was perfect.

I have a passel of friends at COLOR Creative in Seattle—the best doggone creative agency in the Seattle area—who were instrumental storytelling partners. I can't possibly name everyone I worked with, but they are all exceptional. Elie Goral and Paul Mandeville have been story buddies for years and years and years, and they never disappoint. When Chad Cobain joined the team, I found his work to be just as stellar. Sarah Xanthakis whipped up my website, designed the logo and illustrations, and put her stamp on my brand.

And what can I say about the Dream Team? Alex Stowe (Director), Ty Migota (Director of Photography), and Jess Grant (Producer) brought their immense skills to the table to deliver exquisite videos. There is no one I would rather work with on a story. Plus, they're a ton of fun on a shoot.

There are so many others. Heather S. Alabado is the very epitome of a Creative Director. Her eye for art direction and animation is exceptional. Landin Williams's editing skills are legendary. His eye (and ear) for detail are amazing. I could not have done my job without all of the creative talents around me.

And finally, thank you to my clients. I won't name names here, but you know who you are. Thank you for the opportunity to step in to your business, work closely with your customers, and break down a few barriers along the way.

# ENDNOTES

1 Chris Sclafani, "A Case Study Primer: Origins and basic Principles," *Global Journal of Human-Social Science: Linguistics & Education* 17, no. 3 (2017): 1, https://globaljournals.org/ GJHSS_Volume17/4-A-Case-Study-Primer-Origins.pdf

2 Content Marketing Institute, *B2B Content Marketing 2020* (October 2019), 24, https://contentmarketinginstitute.com/ wp-content/uploads/2019/10/2020_B2B_Research_Final.pdf

3 Dr. Janet Fitzakerley, "Cortical Language Areas," Speech and Language, University of Minnesota Medical School Duluth, March 4, 2015, https://www.d.umn.edu/~jfitzake/Lectures/DMED/ SpeechLanguage/CorticalS_LAreas/CorticalLanguageAreas.html

4 Diane Pecher, Inge Boot, and Saskia Van Dantzig, "Abstract Concepts: Sensory-Motor Grounding, Metaphors, and Beyond," *Psychology of Learning and Motivation* 54 (2011): 217, https:// globaljournals.org/GJHSS_Volume17/4-A-Case-Study-Primer- Origins.pdf

5 Emory News Center, "Hearing metaphors activates sensory brain regions," Woodruff Health Sciences Center, February, 2012, http://news.emory.edu/stories/2012/02/metaphor_brain_ imaging/

6   Raymond Mar and Keith Oatley, "The Function of Fiction Is the Abstraction and Simulation of Social Experience," *Perspectives on Psychological Science* (May 1, 2008): 173, accessed June 24, 2021, National Library of Medicine, https://journals.sagepub.com/doi/abs/10.1111/j.1745-6924.2008.00073.x?journalCode=ppsa.

7   Nadine Gogolla, "The Insular Cortex," *Current Biology* 27, no. 12 (June 2017): 173, accessed June 24, 2021, https://doi.org/10.1016/j.cub.2017.05.010

8   Annie Murphy Paul, "Your Brain on Fiction," New York Times, March 17, 2012, https://www.nytimes.com/2012/03/18/opinion/sunday/the-neuroscience-of-your-brain-on-fiction.html?pagewanted=all

9   George J. Stephens, Lauren J. Silbert, and Uri Hasson, "Speaker-listener Neural Coupling Underlies Successful Communication," Proceedings of the National Academy of Sciences of the United States of America, August 10, 2010, https://doi.org/10.1073/pnas.1008662107.

10  Alice LaPlante, *The Making of a Story: A Norton Guide to Creative Writing* (New York: W. W. Norton & Company, 2007), 24.

11  Adam Grant, *Originals: How Non-conformists Move the World* (New York: Penguin Books, 2017), 221-22.

12  Ibid.

13  Danny Donchev, "37 Mind Blowing YouTube Facts, Figures and Statistics - 2021," FortuneLords, July 9, 2021, https://fortunelords.com/youtube-statistics.

14  Tom Cochrane, "Life is a Highway," on *Mad Mad World* (1991).

15  xyzowl, "The State of Video Marketing 2021," https://www.
    wyzowl.com/state-of-video-marketing-2021-report/.

16  Donchev, "37 Mind Blowing YouTube Facts," https://fortune
    lords.com/youtube-statistics.

17  vidyard, "2021 Video in Business Benchmark Report," accessed
    February 11, 2021, https://www.vidyard.com/business-video-
    benchmarks/.